PRAISE FOR CARRIE DICKIE

"Carrie's caring yet firm approach as a business coach was literally the difference between success and failure for me in this profession. Her mentorship changed my life and the lives of my family."

— Mark Gordon, cardiologist turned
professional network marketer

"Carrie's integrity, passion for people, and candor, coupled with her training skills provide the average person the principles to achieve above average results in business and in life."

— Stu Brodie, thirty year network marketing veteran

"I have worked with Carrie for over 20 years. Her dedication to others shines through her intensely joyful heart. Carrie's warm, fun authenticity connects her to her audiences. She has been a true mentor and my extraordinary friend. Carrie Dickie is the real deal!"

— Cherise Matthews,
fitness coach and 25 year professional networker

"Carrie Dickie is the epitome of love-based leadership. Her heart shines through every call, every conversation, and every keynote. Once that woman steps on stage, watch out! Magic ensues. Her energy is captivating!"

— Rachel Jackson, serial entrepreneur

Network Marketing

The View from Venus

Network Marketing: The View from Venus

Published by Pure Joy Press

San Clemente, CA

Library of Congress Control Number: 2016937239

Dickie, Carrie, Author

Network Marketing: The View from Venus

Carrie Dickie

ISBN: 978-0-9974590-0-5

BUSINESS & ECONOMICS / Marketing / Multilevel

SELF-HELP / Personal Growth / Success

QUANTITY PURCHASES: Schools, companies, professional groups, clubs, and other organizations may qualify for special terms when ordering quantities of this title. For information, email carrie@carriedickie.com.

Network Marketing

The View from Venus

A manual for men and women who want
to elevate the great profession of network marketing

CARRIE DICKIE

ACKNOWLEDGMENTS

I WOULD LIKE TO THANK my beautiful and talented friends and business partners who have inspired me to encapsulate my working knowledge of the network marketing profession in the form of this book. Without our stumbles and falls, our giant steps forward and our all-out "wins", I wouldn't have had the desire or the fuel to create this work.

Additionally, I am in deep gratitude to Jim and Anna Locke for walking each step of the way with me, reminding me that what I was writing was relevant and required. Thank you, Jim, for being my very first partner in this endeavor.

Thank you to my Mom and Dad for reading my work and for teaching me *how* to work. If I hadn't learned tenacity from you, I assure you this book would never have come to fruition.

Thank you, Sandee Crane, for questioning every single word of my manuscript with your red pencil. I know you lost a few weeks of your life, and I am very grateful. Tawny, thank you for knowing me, and for removing anything that was "not Carrie" that I picked up along the way. The book is truly mine because of you.

Thank you to Diane Mullins, Polly Letofsky, and Christina Rosenberg for taking me to the finish line when I felt like giving up.

Last, thank you to my husband, partner, and best friend, Gordon, for always seeing me and supporting me in all that I do. For you I am richly blessed.

THE WORLD HAS SHIFTED. FISCAL responsibility, intro-spection, and personal responsibility are the order of the day. People are re-evaluating. They are calling on God to clean up their lives. Venus is on the rise, and Mars is taking a well-deserved break.

Network marketing is coming of age. Still in its infancy, this profession is the fast track to personal growth. Most choose to exit, as the path is too daunting. Others push through and move through the fear and darkness, confident that the light on the other side is brilliant and shining just for them. People are being called on a soul level to live a bigger life.

You are being summoned to step into your greatness. You have been given the keys to wealth and freedom, and the keys to yourself. Come with me. Take a risk and follow your heart. Open your mind and believe there is more.

It will be challenging and exhilarating. It will infuse your soul with light and passion. You will learn to love people as they are. You will learn to love yourself. You just may find inner peace.

Will you choose it?

Will you walk within?

Will you venture to Venus?

Preface

I WROTE THIS BOOK BECAUSE I have a burning desire to see millions of people succeed in network marketing, the profession that has set my family free. Before network marketing, I never earned more than $40,000 in any calendar year. Today I am blessed to earn a seven-figure annual income.

I graduated from the University of Colorado in 1985 with a Bachelor of Science degree in Advertising. I put myself through school waiting tables, bartending, teaching fitness classes, and selling books door to door. I also worked as a fund-raiser. I joined my first company in 1993 and was captured by the idea of residual income. As in any profession, it can take a few companies to find the right fit. I worked with two more before I earned my first million in 2008. I was blessed to find my "home" in 2010.

In these pages, I start from day one and give you what you need to build a multimillion-dollar organization with thousands of people all over the world. I teach you what to do and how to do it. I give you the meat on the bones. I share the nuts and bolts. I teach you how to set goals. I empower you with the invites I use with my friends, family, and prospects. I share details about my presentation and how to set up an effective three-way call. I help you avoid pitfalls by teaching you what not to do. I share how I develop leaders. I show you how to build a business that will last. I promise I get real and tell the truth about what it takes. I am excited to have given you all the secrets I use to build my business with heart, passion, and a sense of humor. Join me. Let's do this for *you*!

PRELUDE
(A JOURNAL ENTRY)

IT'S JULY 29, 2012, AND I'm flying in a plane, enjoying the view from thirty thousand feet. I am feeling insignificant and totally connected. I'm flying above the cotton candy clouds where the sun is always shining. There are no stop signs and no traffic. There are no limits of any kind. This is total freedom and infinite possibility, a place where all I can see is the bigger picture.

These are the last few minutes of the flight, and the view is magnificent. Each cloud seems to be independent yet connected to the one beside it, a virtual trampoline of cotton balls begging to be jumped upon. I wonder if it is time. The book—most of it, anyway—has been traveling within me for a while now. It seems that the last pieces of the puzzle have fallen into place. The book feels complete.

I don't make big decisions anymore without checking in. So

I ask, "God, should I carve out an hour each day to write, even though I'm still building my business, raising the boys, staying physically fit, and trying to put the occasional meal on the table? If so, give me a sign." It is a simple request, and the answer is immediate. We enter a mass of clouds, and I can no longer see anything. Instead of being above them, I am in them. I am blinded by the white. In an instant, I think I have my answer. "Nope, it's not time yet." I close my eyes, and I'm secretly relieved. There is so much on my plate right now. Maybe it will be simpler to get started next year when the kids are a little older and my business is more established. Yet when I open my eyes again, there, outside my window, is the most beautiful tiny rainbow. It gleams in the midst of the clouds for me. I realize this is my real answer, a perfect, clear, and simple "Yes, the time is now."

Gordon is lost in his own heaven, his music. I interrupt. I pull off his headphones and point to the rainbow. I am looking through both of our windows, and it is clear and bright. He tells me he cannot see it. Then it's gone. It is visible for ten seconds and no more.

It is time. I have my answer. The world is ready, and I am too. The book inside me will be born, *Network Marketing: The View from Venus.*

The above journal entry was written two years and three months before I wrote the very first word of this book. After that flight ended, I did not think of starting my book again until the first week of November 2014, when I picked up a book by Steven Pressfield called *The War of Art: Break Through the Blocks and Win Your*

Inner Creative Battles (2002). This book had been on my shelf for years, patiently waiting to be read.

I read the following paragraph from Pressfield and started writing my book the very next day:

WHAT I KNOW

There's a secret that real writers know that "wannabe" writers don't, and the secret is this: It's not the writing part that's hard. What's hard is sitting down to write. What keeps us from sitting down is resistance.

Pressfield goes on to say more:

Procrastination is the most common manifestation of resistance because it's the easiest to rationalize. We don't tell ourselves, "I'm never going to write my symphony." Instead we say, "I'm going to write my symphony; I'm just going to start tomorrow."

If I had not picked up Pressfield's book, I imagine my own symphony would still be inside me, longing to be written.

Introduction

I AM A PROFESSIONAL NETWORK marketer. I was born to do it. It took me fifty-two years to understand that network marketing held the keys to my destiny. Perhaps it holds the keys to yours, too. Perhaps it will change the course of your life forever, just like it did mine.

There have been many "whys" along my twenty-two-year business journey, but none has burned hotter than the two-part why, or reason, that burns in my heart today. It's simple. The first part of my why is for you. I yearn to help you build a strong and powerful network marketing organization that will create passive, residual income that will continue with or without you. Whether you have a strong sponsor or no sponsor; whether you are experienced or a newcomer; whether you are a teenager or retired; I want to fill your toolbox with the tools that I have used to build a powerful network of men and women, a network of committed people who are successful like me, because they are passionate about this work. I want to welcome you to join us.

Even though the first part of my why sounds like it's for you, it is really for all of us. I am determined to transform the great profession of network marketing, and I cannot do it alone. You are necessary for me to realize the second part of my why. If I can help you become a viable network marketer, my job becomes easier. Shifting the profession is my duty, my calling, and the reason that I speak to people every single day about this "road less traveled". It pains me to hear the questions that people ask and the tone in which they ask them. "Is this one of those pyramid schemes?" "Is this one of those things where you sign up and get your friends and neighbors to sign up under you, so you can make a ton of money off them? If this is another multi-level marketing opportunity, I'm not interested. I don't want to sell things to my friends." I'm irritated daily by statements such as "My sister-in-law's brother tried network marketing once, and it didn't work for him."

Indeed, scores of people have given our profession a bad name. Network marketing amateurs are famous for overpromising and under delivering, especially in the areas of potential income and the time that will be required to create large checks. New network marketers are often overzealous and full of enthusiasm and passion for their business enterprise, with few tools and little know-how to support them. Others will hammer their family members and close friends and beg them to join their network marketing company, forgetting that they have offered them three opportunities in the past.

Like them, I have made plenty of mistakes in my two-decade journey to success in this remarkable profession. However, I never considered throwing the baby out with the bathwater. For many years I have been searching for an army of talented and committed leaders and diamonds in the rough who want to join me in elevating this profession. I am passionate about raising its reputation.

You see, if it were not for network marketing, I would not be free. By the time you finish this book, you will understand exactly what freedom does and does not mean to me. It may be a perspective that you have never heard before. I hope it is one that will resonate with you, because the job of improving network marketing's image is a massive one that I cannot accomplish on my own.

To put it simply, I want people of every age, race, color, creed, political affiliation, gender, and religious and sexual orientation to read these words. I want you to learn how to do network marketing with heart, integrity, and passion. It is my fervent desire to help you build a network marketing dynasty that will increase your self-confidence and influence in your community, as well as in the world. Why? So that you can join *me* in my mission of offering time and financial freedom to those trailblazers who are willing to *work for it*, as well as enhance the integrity of the business model that creates it.

In this book, I will share my network marketing journey with you. I will tell you how I found it, how I fell down again and again, making every mistake in the book, and how I picked myself up every single time. I will share how I developed the required skills and honed my talent for *seeing people, loving them*, and *leading them to their brilliance.*

I'm not concerned with which company you are aligned. What really matters is how you represent our profession, build your team, and cooperate with others on the same journey, and how much heart you bring to the table. You see, if we are going to transform network marketing, we need to use more than the Mars mentality. If you want to incorporate the *heart* that is required to build a lasting business, the *joy* that is available, and the *integrity* that this profession lacks, I will need to earn your trust by first explaining the basics. Then I intend to inspire you to *want* to join me in my quest to be the change this profession needs.

Welcome to my perspective of our world and its potential.

Welcome to the ride of your life.

Welcome to the *view from Venus.*

A PRAYER FOR GUIDANCE

Dear Glorious Venus Energy,

It is time. The world is ready for you *and* so is the great profession of network marketing. Transformation is necessary, and you are not only invited but *urged* to help us manifest the shift.

Peace—you are the balm that heals.
Light—you are the medicine of the soul.
Truth—you are the antidote to disease.
Love—you diffuse all fear.

I invite you to come join my friends and me. We have been playing in the basement, and what fun we have had. Recently the roof blew off, and now we are ready to live large. We invite your presence as we join hands and hearts. We celebrate the manifestation of grace, joy, and gratitude. The party is about to begin in network marketing.

Thank you in advance for the healing that is infusing our hearts, minds, and souls. We embrace your precious and timely arrival.

1

MARTIANS AND VENUSIANS DEFINED

BEFORE I CONFUSE TOO MANY of my readers, I want to define the Mars mentality that I see as so prevalent in the network marketing profession. First, this has nothing to do with gender. I love men. I am married to a man. I have two beautiful sons, sixteen and eighteen, who captivate me with their willingness to help, their love of family, and the joy they carry in their hearts.

Back to the Mars mentality—here's how I see it. By the way, I have spent only a few moments researching the planet itself. This is only my perception, a metaphor I have quietly used for more than two decades while building my businesses. Although I have read John Gray's book *Men Are from Mars, Women Are from Venus* (1992), I am not plagiarizing his work. These are simply my unabridged thoughts that come from a life of learning to live authentically as a strong feminine voice in a chorus of (frequently) loud masculine voices.

Here is a quote about Mars from Wikipedia: "In Greek my-thology, Mars is the God of War. Mars lacks active plate tectonics and at present there is no evidence of motion or movement. There are very strong winds and vast dust storms that engulf the entire planet for months." The way I see it, there is zero flexibility on Mars. Mars is rigid. Mars is cloudy, confusing, chaotic, and disor-ganized. Mars is for Martians, not network marketers.

I also read that Mars, because of its red color, is sometimes referred to as "the red planet". Just an aside: According to a body of research called MBS (Manage by Strengths), a direct person (red) focuses on getting results and being in control, and loves a challenge. They are usually outspoken, analytical, self-confident, and often self-made people. Reds want people to get to the point, tie things to results, and make a decision. These are fantastic quali-ties, and quite necessary for building a successful business in any profession. However, they are not *all* the qualities a person must develop to maintain and grow a sizable and sustainable organiza-tion that is healthy, expanding, and full of joy.

By contrast, let's take a look at Venus. I read more from Wiki-pedia: "Venus, the second planet from the sun, is named for the Roman goddess of love and beauty. Venus is the only planet named after a woman. She may have been named for the most beautiful deity of the pantheon because she was the brightest of the five planets known to ancient astronomers. In ancient times, Venus was often thought to be two different stars, the evening star and the morning star, the ones that first appeared at sunrise and sunset.

Venus is the hottest planet in our solar system. Although Venus is not the planet closest to the sun, its dense atmosphere traps heat in a runaway version of the greenhouse effect that warms our earth. As a result, temperatures on Venus reach 870 degrees Fahrenheit, more than hot enough to melt lead. With conditions on Venus that could be described as infernal, Lucifer, the ancient name for Venus, may seem to be more appropriate. However, this name did not carry any fiendish connotations. Lucifer means "light-bringer," and when seen from Earth, Venus is brighter than any other planet or any star in the night sky because of its highly reflective clouds and proximity to our planet."

Wow! Now, that is a perspective from which to build a business. So often, we pumped-up networkers run around telling each other that we are on fire with enthusiasm. We know in our hearts that we are building a bridge to our freedom, and it is for this that we are burnin' up with passion and excitement. Many times the ecstatic phone calls and spur-of-the-moment celebrations have little to do with our own successes and everything to do with those of another.

In summary, the Mars mentality is characterized by ego, fear, jealousy, and lack. It is cold on Mars, not hot. It is all business on Mars; there is no warm and fuzzy there. People fall into line or they fall out. There is no room for deviation or innovation. From my perspective, integrity is probably in question when it is inconvenient. Morals and values are not always a priority on Mars.

Be clear, the Mars mentality is not a distinction between the way men and women build this business. Unfortunately there are plenty of women who show up as "Martians" when they enter the network marketing workforce. Conversely, I have met some of the finest male Venusians that have ever walked planet Earth. They are the most principled and passionate people beside whom I have had the pleasure to work.

Venusians are all heart—open, honest, and peaceful—although you may not see it at first glance. Venusians operate from love, not fear. Venusians check their egos at the door and recognize there is a giant piece of the pie that they "don't know they don't know". Venusians know that network marketing is not a zero sum game and that there is enough for all earnest participants. Venusians operate from abundance and not lack. Venusians are joyful and celebrate the wins of others, although sometimes with quiet exuberance. Some Venusians are reserved; the passion and love just burns in their hearts and in their eyes. Venusians subscribe to the TTSP philosophy (This Too Shall Pass) and recognize that getting too stressed out is not good for a person's health. A Venusian is hopeful and ready for the next great thing to happen in their business. They will also feel and overcome the frequent stings of disappointment. A Venusian recognizes that they are not "the deal" and that other people are. Hugging a Venusian is addictive because their energy ignites the spirit. Venusians are poised and graceful, radiant and filled with gratitude. Writing about them makes me long to be a better person—a better mother, wife, friend, and network marketer.

Martians and Venusians cannot be distinguished by gender. Nor can they be identified at first glance. It can take days, weeks, months, or in some cases even years to determine from which planet a person's mentality originates. Here is what is beautiful.

Any Martian can decide to adopt the Venusian mentality at any time, for any reason. We each get to decide for ourselves which planet we represent!

LET'S GET STARTED!

I made you a promise. I told you that I am going to share my perspective on how to build a successful network marketing business. I am beyond excited to do it. I will share all the secrets I know. I will tell you every mistake I have made along the way so that you can avoid making them. I must warn you, however, that you will probably make many of these same mistakes anyway. I underscore again that there is always that piece of the pie that you don't know that you don't know. I can only hope that my piece of that pie has gotten a bit smaller in the last twenty-two years and that, with this effort, I will be able to put some meat on the network marketing bones and offer some ideas for you to chew on. It is always my hope to be of service to you and to anyone wanting residual income and the freedom of time that comes with it. If that is what you are looking for, plus some self-love, expansion of knowledge, and personal development, then you are in the right place at the right time.

As we begin our journey together, I will share the short story of my introduction to network marketing, of my being in the right place at the right time. I did not think I was looking for anything when the profession of network marketing came knocking at my door in the form of Larry Blather. He was there to meet with my husband, Gordon. I had a business and I was working my own hours. I loved what I was doing and did not know that I had the ability to earn more income. I was in a happy place. I was building a fund-raising business with my mom. We had fun every day, laughed and laughed, helped people, and made a difference every time we went to work.

When Larry knocked, I answered my door and told him, "I'm so sorry. Gordon left a few minutes ago. You just missed him. Did he know you were coming?"

Larry said, "Well, yes, we had an appointment. I was supposed to show him my new business."

I felt horrible. I asked him, "How about I make you a cup of tea and you can show it to me? Then I will tell him all about it later."

Larry came inside and proceeded to share all the details of his new venture selling vitamins. Truthfully, I didn't hear much of his presentation, and this guy was hardly the picture of health. I did hear enough to ask, "So you're telling me that someone sells vitamins in Kentucky or Oklahoma and I get paid?"

Larry replied, "That's exactly what I'm telling you."

I responded without hesitation, "Then sign me up!" When Gordon got home an hour or so later, I exclaimed, "Honey, we have a new business!"

This was my introduction to the concept of person-to-person distribution, better known as network marketing. I didn't know then that network marketing was nothing more than word-of-mouth advertising, that it would change the direction of my life, that I would be in and out of it, that I would be furious with this business model, mesmerized by it, that I would never be able to walk away from it, that it was in my blood, and that I was wired for it. I did not know that my assignment was going to be much bigger than just building a network. I had no clue that I had been charged, along with many other remarkable and talented men and women, with the enormous task of bringing light to a profession that had been operating in the shadowy edges of our economy.

Venusian? Here we go!

2

SEVEN MYTHS THAT GIVE NETWORK MARKETING A BAD RAP

MYTH NUMBER ONE

"It's easy! You just enroll a few people
and they build it for you!"

IF ANYONE TELLS YOU THIS, they are mistaken. Network
marketing is not a get-rich-quick scheme. In any country, in any
language, in any business, anything worth having is worth working
for. Network marketing is no different. If they tell you, "Just enroll
and we'll build it," they are pulling your leg. Unless you are serious about building a part-time, full-time, or big-time business in
network marketing, just become a customer and use the products.
Some of the very finest products on the planet are moved through
person-to-person distribution. No matter what anyone says, you

cannot build a business in your spare time. It just will not pay you. Network marketing is like real estate, mortgage brokerage, or insurance, because you must make a reasonable investment of time to see any sustainable results.

MYTH NUMBER TWO

"You can have time and financial freedom
in just a couple of years!"

This, also, is simply not true. Building a network requires skill, perseverance, and time. If you are not all in, don't get in. This is not a business for the weak of heart. Network marketing has a learning curve, just like any other business, and you will need to ride it. The good news is that you do not have to wait until you are skilled to get started. You can earn in this profession while you learn, and typically, the person who enrolled you is dying to see you succeed.

One of my mentors said it best: "People overestimate what can happen in one to two years in network marketing, but they dramatically underestimate what can happen in three to five." I would add only one thought. That first five years must be full of personal growth and action and not just activity. Action is being in front of people, sharing your business in a consistent way, and having business partners to validate you. (We will cover this later.) Action is not cleaning your office, getting set up with the latest phone or computer—getting ready to get ready. Do not confuse activity with action. Action means you are on the edge of your comfort zone; you are growing by learning and doing new things.

You are uncomfortable. You are making mistakes, and you are doing all of this on the phone or face-to-face with potential business partners. You must plan, do, check, and adjust at all times. You are constantly evaluating your performance and results. Nothing will build your skill set faster. If you are blessed enough to have a mentor, ask them to hold you accountable and beg them to be honest about your shortcomings and your strengths. In this way, your first two years will serve as a valuable foundation on which to build your business. Always remember—you will be bad before you're good and good before you're great.

Please note what I'm about to say, because it is vitally important. You may or may not see much money at this stage. You may feel terribly underpaid for the time and energy you have invested. The speed with which your organization builds will depend, in large part, upon the skill set and list of contacts you have at the beginning of your network marketing journey. Skills and talents from other business endeavors transfer and can shorten your learning curve dramatically. If you have been a real estate broker or a salesman, a human resources manager, or a retail store manager, chances are good that you already have learned a thing or two about leading and motivating people.

If you have been an entrepreneur and owned your own business, you may know exactly how to get up and get going. You may know that the buck stops with you, and you may clearly understand the mantra, "If it's going to be, it's up to me." Conversely, if you have been an employee who punches a time clock; works an eight-hour shift each day; and receives a paycheck, a 401(k), and a W-2, this is going to be a very different adventure. You need to recognize that you are training for a brand new career. Be an optimistic realist and commit to your new business openly and with enthusiasm. Remember you are getting paid—albeit minimally at first—while learning and building your skills and business. For goodness' sake, nobody pays you during the four years that it takes to get through college.

MYTH NUMBER THREE

"Network marketing is a scam!"

I checked out Webster's online definition of a *scam*. A scam is "an instance of the use of dishonest methods to acquire something of value" (www.merriam-webster.com/thesaurus/scam). Network marketing hardly fits the bill, though I have a pretty good idea why it has been mistakenly categorized as such for decades. You see, the upside potential is huge, and there is virtually no barrier to entry. Seems to be too good to be true, right? Let me explain.

Network marketing is growing by leaps and bounds, and it even has an organization called the Direct Selling Association (DSA) to legitimize it. According to the DSA website, the DSA was formed in 1900 to "look after the needs of direct selling companies and create an image for direct selling as a respectable profession". The DSA is the national trade association of the leading firms that manufacture and distribute goods and services sold directly to consumers. Approximately two hundred companies are members of the DSA, including many well-known brand names. The

DSA's mission is "To protect, serve, and promote the effectiveness of member companies and the independent business people they represent. To ensure that the marketing by member companies of products and/or the direct sales opportunity is conducted with the highest level of business ethics and service to consumers." (www. dsa.org) That does not sound like a scam to me. Let's take a closer look.

After years in this profession, I have a keen understanding of why and how network marketing has been misunderstood for decades. Network marketing falls under attack, in part, because the barrier to entry is so low. Since the products that are moved through networks are often in high demand, the cost to join most network marketing companies is less than $1,000, and the upside potential is virtually unlimited. People flock to join. In the United States alone, about 165,000 people are joining a network marketing company each week. Almost anybody can come up with the investment to get started and they do. The DSA website (http://www.dsa.org/) reports that "The 2013 estimated retail sales of $32.67 billion for the direct selling channel were up 3.3 percent in the United States; from $31.63 billion in 2012. The U.S. market increase of 3.3 percent in 2013 continued an upward trend that began after 2009 and brought the profession to a record high." It goes on to say, "The size of the direct selling sales force increased 5.7 percent to 16.8 million people in 2013—a record high."

So why is there all the fuss? Here are my thoughts. Since almost anyone can get in, many people find the money and join. They hear the *potential* for success and they begin to dream. They get in touch with their wants and desires that have been locked away for years or even decades. For a brief moment, they picture themselves earning more money, buying a bigger home, and driving a better car. They see themselves exercising more, working less, and spending more time with their loved ones and friends. For a short period of time, they believe network marketing will save them. And to be completely honest, there are those network marketing "unprofessionals" who fuel that fire of illusion. They overpromise and under deliver. They themselves are not yet experienced, but they exaggerate their success and their earnings. This is absolutely true and something I hope to change as I elevate the way this profession presents itself to the world.

I urge you to remember that we are all adults. We must all learn to take personal responsibility for our business decisions. It is important to be realistic. You see, it is really all about expectations. For example, nobody would start college and expect to receive a degree after their freshman year. That would be absurd. Everyone knows it takes at least four years to receive a degree. Nobody would start dental school and expect to be a dentist earning a full-time income in one or two years. Nor would an entrepreneur predict massive earning results in real estate, insurance, or mortgage lending in such a short time. Most people expect to put years of sweat equity into these business endeavors before creating a full-time income to support themselves and their families.

Back to network marketing: the barrier to entry is quite low, so people join all the time with massive goals backed by little action. They pay their money, and instead of going to "school" to get educated on Monday, they go to the gym. Their belief in the company, its products, and its people may be quite high, but their belief in themselves may be very, very low. Often they will keep the starter package because they are excited about the products it contains, but without making the effort to get education in the form of on-the-job training, their dream of a business is all but dead and they don't even realize it. They join, they pay money, they dream, and then they are out. Unfortunately the flame of discontent has been stoked, resulting in disappointment and lack of confidence, and they quit. This is what they remember the next time someone offers them a network marketing opportunity or shares that they have discovered a new one for themselves. They cannot help but turn up their noses and say, "Network marketing is a scam. I tried it and it did not work for me."

I know this to be true. Network marketing does work when you work it, but it is not called "net-wish marketing" or "net-play marketing". It takes work, it takes time, and it has highs and lows. You will experience wins and losses, and you will stumble, fall, and fall again. I tell people every day, "Just be sure you are falling forward." Network marketing is an arena in which an average person with above-average passion, authenticity, tenacity, belief, and commitment, as well as above-average work ethic can succeed beyond their wildest dreams. I know. I have done it. If this little girl from Colorado, who never made more than $40,000 in any calendar year, can do it, then so can you. Nobody said it was going to be easy. As I explained in the last chapter, if someone tells you that, they are wrong.

MYTH NUMBER FOUR

"You must be an extrovert or a super-salesperson
to achieve success in network marketing."

Network marketing has super-salespeople; extroverts who have never met a stranger and who could sell sand in Arizona. However, I have learned over the last two decades that network marketers come in all shapes, sizes, ages, and personality types. Because of this variety, it is impossible to pick out the rock stars at first glance. There is no such thing as a typical network marketer. Even shy, quiet, and introverted people enjoy great success in this profession.

I have learned that you really never know who is going to join you in your business. Because network marketing is not for the faint of heart, it is not an easy business. It is simple, but it is not easy. After years in the profession, I have discovered that "The ones you think will, won't while the ones you think won't, will." Every rule has the occasional exception.

I know this for sure. Most people are never going to enroll with you to build a network marketing business. It is all about timing, facing fear, and being willing to step into a life-altering business endeavor. The new person recognizes that entering network marketing has lots of potential. They also sense, but usually will not acknowledge, that they don't know what they don't know. Once they begin to experience the fear of failure and rejection and the steep learning curve, many will pull out. It is human nature to avoid pain. It takes a rare and fearless person to move into it.

Additionally, most people simply do not have the staying power. I have a mentor who says, "Commitment is doing what you said you were going to do, long after the desire to do it has left you." Most people do not fully integrate this philosophy into their lives. Statistics say that a person who joins you today is not likely to be with you next year. You cannot necessarily look at someone and know what is in their heart. Engaging in network marketing is not about how a person shows up on the outside; it is about what is burning within them.

If you have done your job right and educated people about the merits of your remarkable product line, they will at least continue to use the products and remain on auto-ship. If your Company has programs in place that are designed to retain customers, you can build a business that will last a lifetime. As an example, some distributors in my business show up at every meeting and event. They take notes and socialize with friends. They are positive and happy to be there, and they never bring a prospect with them. I have absolutely no issue with this. I am delighted to have them. I recognize that these distributors are our customers and they come for the fun, the energy, and the community. These people are the proverbial bread and butter of our business, and I care very much for each and every one of them.

So the myth that says, "You must be an extrovert or a super-salesperson to have success in network marketing" is not true. I would suggest that most successful network marketers are introverts who have adopted some extroverted characteristics. They are wired to be connectors, but not in an overt way. They are often very comfortable one-on-one, and they do not always have the desire or need to be the center of attention. I came to earth wired to have fun, laughter, and joy in my interactions with others. By age five, that innocent joie de vivre was socialized out of me and I was insecure, anxious, and self-conscious. I was terrified to be in front of the room. It took me more than forty years to remember who I am at my core—who I came here to be, what I came here to do, and that it was *true* for me to show up every day as a Venusian: to be present and ready to play, and to remember that I am *more than enough*.

This is what I want you to know. You can be whoever you are and build a successful network marketing business. Here's the deal, though: You will need to become the best you possible to be a happy and fulfilled network marketer. You will need to develop grace and gratitude, and learn to manage your ego. When you do this and understand that your personal and business growth is directly proportional to how much you help others grow and prosper, you will achieve great satisfaction. If you hold on to the notion that it is all about you, then whatever you gain through your successful network marketing business will still leave you lacking. It simply will not be fulfilling for you.

MYTH NUMBER FIVE

"Anyone can do network marketing."

Success in network marketing requires three things. First and foremost, there must be a genuine *desire for change*. This point cannot be overstated. I am not suggesting that this desire is necessarily evident from the start. It may be a subconscious desire when you are first exposed to the network marketing opportunity. You may play around with this business in the beginning, with no big goals or dreams burning in your heart. However, to have huge success, the yearning for change will eventually consume you. This desire is a must-have to face the challenges you will encounter in building your business. Having that desire is wonderful, though. It is a gift to be in touch with it and to work every day on purpose. It is what keeps you passionately engaged in the game of life.

A desire to change some aspect of your life, however, is not enough. The second requirement for success in network marketing is to *be open and coachable*. Network marketing is simple, not easy, and it is unlike anything you have ever done before. Following the proven system, and not introducing a new one, is your job. No matter how much business experience you have, being an astute observer and following those who have gone before you is vital. Most people are not conscious enough to check their egos at the door. Listen actively and intently. Ask good questions and follow the leaders' examples. The presumption, of course, is that you trust the company and the people who have come before you. If you don't trust them, why would you even start? I propose that all can choose this, but that not everyone will. Arrogant know-it-all types who show up with their own ideas about how to build their business usually don't last very long. They are in and out. Being a humble and motivated learner is a huge benefit in network marketing.

Imperative to your success in network marketing are having a desire to change your life and being coachable and teachable.

The third requirement is having a *stellar work ethic*. Without it, the other two requirements mean nothing. Being committed to going the distance is critical. Adopting the mind-set that "if it's going to be, it's up to me" is crucial as well. Deciding "I will until" is easy to say, but not so easy to remember when the going gets tough. Staying focused and doing something every single day to move your business forward is essential to the success you seek. Lazy people do not stand a chance in our profession, and they weed themselves out quickly.

So can anyone be successful at network marketing? Yes, I presume anyone is able, but only if they choose the prerequisites shared above. Some people have a desire for their lives to be different. Some people are good students and will listen to suggestions and feedback. Some people go the extra mile in whatever work they do. It is a rare bird that has all three. However, these are the people whom you are seeking to join your business team, people who are ready to take full responsibility for everything they have manifested in their lives thus far, and for everything they choose to usher into their lives in the future. Most people choose the path of least resistance. It is sad but true, and is just what the evidence shows to be the case.

MYTH NUMBER SIX

"Products moved through network marketing
are more expensive."

This is generally not true. Network marketing products are no
more expensive than any others. What differs is the distribution
of profits. Think about a tube of lipstick from Nordstrom or a basketball from Big Five Sporting Goods. The end consumer pays a
price for each of these products that is much higher than the cost
of production. When you consider the raw materials necessary in
the making of these two products, it is easy to guess that the cost
of manufacturing is not very high.

Many layers are involved in getting these products to the end
user, and each layer has an added cost. It starts with the design of
the product, then the raw materials, and the cost of manufacturing the product. There are salaries, rent, overhead, insurance, and
utilities, just to mention a few. Then there are the most expensive
layers: marketing, advertising, sales forces, sales training, and distribution networks. The sum of these layers establishes the manufacturer's cost; plus the manufacturer adds its own profit margin to
arrive at the final sale price.

Although this is a somewhat oversimplified, in a typical network marketing business model, the manufacturer (the Company)
reduces their overall cost (i.e., their sales price) by eliminating expenses associated with employing and training a sales force. Their
advertising expenses are also significantly reduced. Since word-of-

mouth advertising (the cornerstone of network marketing) is essentially free, distributors who have paid to join the Company's network marketing team are the Company's resources. Furthermore, especially in the age of the Internet, the Company can significantly reduce its distribution costs by consolidating its inventory in a few locations, as the order fulfillment process is fully automated. These cost savings for the Company are then passed on to the distributor organization in the form of commissions, bonuses, and other incentives. Additionally, the Company is able to reap cash flow benefits by being paid before the product is even shipped. This is a definite plus for a company using the network marketing business model in today's financially pressured world.

In the final analysis, for products that have a story to tell, where the complexity and cost of advertising would be huge, the network marketing business model is more efficient and effective. Open your mouth, share what you love, move people to make a decision to buy, and both you and the Company get paid. Beautiful! Fair! Genius!

Note: An excellent resource for a better understanding of the network marketing business model in general can be found in the work of Robert Kiyosaki, *The Business of the 21st Century*, 2012. Both paperback and audio versions are available online at Amazon.com.

MYTH NUMBER SEVEN

"The people at the top make all the money
in network marketing."

Timing matters in building your network marketing business. It does. Timing is always important in any business, and ours is no exception. I would not be as excited to open a coffee franchise today as I would have been twenty years ago. The window of opportunity has closed a great deal. Similarly, if millions and millions of people recognize the name of your Company and are familiar with the products you represent, you are going to have a harder time building your business. It is important that you join the Company before everyone has heard of it.

That being said, if you are part of a good company that has a fair compensation plan based on hard work, you can absolutely out earn the person who brought you into the business. If you and the people you bring into the business are more effective in the process of duplication, you can earn a bigger check. If you personally develop more leaders and teach more people to teach more people to teach, you can out earn people who joined the company years before you even heard of it. How exciting is that?

It is important to point out that this is not true of all network marketing companies. All compensation plans are not created equally. You need to ask the right questions and investigate the plan before you sign on the dotted line and invest your time and energy in this new opportunity. In a fair compensation plan, your earnings are the result of the effort you put in and your mastery of the system.

One thing I know for sure. Your earnings are not based on the often-subjective opinion of the next-higher-ranking person in the company. No matter where or when you start in a network marketing company, you are, first and foremost, the CEO of your own business. You earn in proportion to how well you build your team and generate revenue for the company. In traditional business, it is pretty safe to assume that a midlevel manager is not likely to out earn his boss. Similarly, a vice president is not going to out earn the CEO. Network marketing levels the playing field. This is the most remarkable system in which I have participated. It does not matter where you have been, what you have done, or how much you previously earned. Everyone starts at the bottom with the potential to earn his or her way to the top.

3

LAYING THE FOUNDATION FOR A VENUS MIND-SET

IT FEELS LIKE THE PERFECT time to lay the foundation on which you can place your network marketing toolbox. If you want to use all the gifts available to you in building a strong and resilient business, you will need to get your head right. The business of network marketing is 10 percent mechanics and 90 percent mind-set. Your success will be in direct proportion to how much you believe in who you are and what you do. Which comes first, the belief or the mechanics? Belief is required to attract people to your business. How do you exude confidence when you are brand new and just starting out?

You do it just like an artist, writer, or athlete. Learn, practice, and repeat. You learn a little bit about it. You talk to people who have gone before you and follow the first few steps laid out for you by your coaches, teachers, or leaders. You are coachable. These steps are explained in detail in future chapters. You read a few short books that will help you understand the basics of network marketing. It is through this process that you learn about the proverbial bulletproof vest that you need to take action effectively and to prosper. Be keenly aware that success is ultimately about action.

If you wanted to be a painter, you would paint, right? If you believed you were a writer, you would take out your laptop and write. If you aspired to be a marathon runner, you would run. We learn through doing, just like any sculptor, author, gymnast, swimmer, football player, or goalkeeper. How funny would it be to see an iron man sitting in an office reading about the art of riding a bike, running, and swimming? Sounds ridiculous, I know. Network marketing is very similar. Unlike real estate, insurance, medicine, or law, you do not go to school for months or years before you can begin to practice your trade. That is why building your confidence, setting proper expectations, learning enough to have a strong presentation at the outset, and establishing the right mind-set are critical to your success.

You will hear me say again and again that this business is very simple but not easy. I cannot stress this point enough. Even if you have been an entrepreneur for your entire career, you must recognize that network marketing is entirely different from any business you have ever done. The good news is that the learning curve is very short. The bad news is that it is very, very steep. The most exciting part is that you can earn while you learn. The faster you learn through action, the more money you will make. This I know for sure.

WHAT YOU NEED AND
WHAT YOU DON'T!

Let's cover a few things you will need to know before you begin and some things you *do not* need to know.

I promise you will not need to understand every detail about the products offered by your Company. Similarly, you will not need to understand your Company's compensation plan in its entirety. I urge you to remember one thing in all that you do: *you are in the business of duplication.* If you think you have to know everything before you get started, then so will everyone you enroll. If you are able to answer every question that comes up when you are sharing with friends or colleagues, they will believe they cannot open their mouths until they are experts. Monkey see, monkey do.

When I am with a potential business partner, I often pick up the phone and have someone *else* answer a question just to model the proper behavior. In network marketing this is referred to as a three-way call. The best way to teach is by example. I say something like "Wow, what a great question. I'm glad you asked. My friend Linda loves to talk about how we make money. Let's see if I can get her on the phone." You can even say something like "What a good question. I do not know, but I will find out the answer right away. There are tons of people we can ask." When you approach their questions this way, the potential business partner is getting a few messages. Number one: "I don't have to do this alone." Number two: "I don't have to know everything to get started." Remember—in network marketing it is not "you go"—it is "we go."

Here is the best part. Unlike in law, medicine, or insurance where hundreds of questions can arise, in network marketing there are only about twenty that come up over and over. In thirty to sixty days of working your business consistently, you will encounter about 90 percent of the questions that will ever be asked. If you wait to build your business until you have all the answers, that example will be duplicated through your entire team. People will believe they should be experts before they ever pick up the phone. Everybody will be getting ready to get ready. They will all be studying, reading, and learning: nobody will be sharing the business or offering product to anyone. This is not how a business grows. It is imperative that you use the three-way call method and share this information without getting bogged down in details.

I offer a couple of easy reads to my new business partners, especially those who are interested in making significant income in network marketing. Because I am a leader, I make these books available to people on the day they sign up. I offer them for the same price I paid, and I make sure that is the lowest price on the market. Again, we are in the business of duplication. I want people to go home and start filling their minds with valid information before they succumb to all the uninformed opinions on network marketing from naysayer friends, family, and associates. I ask them not to share any details about their new business until they have read these books and learned enough to raise their confidence level to support their decision to become a network marketer.

Mark and Rene Reid Yarnell have written a very simple guide that is extremely beneficial. The abridged version of *Your First Year in Network Marketing* (2006) is a realistic account of what you can expect as you set out on your network marketing journey. It will prepare you for the rejection, deception, apathy, and attrition that you are guaranteed to encounter. *The Greatest Networker in the World*, by John Milton Fogg (1997), is a storybook that illustrates the Venus perspective in building a network marketing business. These two books can be read in a day or two and will be tremendously helpful to you in confidently making your first contacts in our profession.

As a network marketing professional, I have copies of these books available to my team. Additionally, I carry training materials from my Company so that I can assign homework right out of the gate. If my new people have training materials in their hands when they leave me after enrolling, they can immediately work on building their confidence on their way home by listening to a CD or book on tape.

It has been my experience that people who enroll with me are only one step closer to fully committing. They are not all in until they take action. I am a firm believer in giving direction in the form of an assignment. This is my opportunity to see if I have a player. I rarely pay much attention to what people say after they pay their money and officially join my business because I have found that talk is cheap. Instead, I watch what people do. I share more about my expectations when we get into the training section of this book.

Numbers are definitely important in network marketing. But to call it a numbers game, as some do, is an oversimplification. I do not resonate with this Martian concept: "Throw it against the wall and see what sticks." You could certainly go through the numbers from year to year and eventually find people who will engage in the business no matter what. But how many "dead bodies" will you leave in your wake? Saying whatever it takes to enroll people in your business, followed by "Give me a call if you have any questions," is not the way to build a strong and sustainable business. One of the biggest problems I see in network marketing is when inexperienced people overpromise and under deliver. I believe we must recognize that hype can be harmful and half-truths can be damaging. Be mindful in building your team. Tell the truth, set realistic expectations, and treat others the way you would have them treat you. Love people and find the best in them. Challenge them to work on their own behalf and to stretch themselves to become the people they have the potential to become.

This is the Venus method of building a business. If we want to shift network marketing, we must be the change we want to see.

DETACHMENT

Now let's talk about a concept that will help you build your business and allow you to live your life in a more joyous way. Sounds good, doesn't it? It is good. It's called detachment, and it will truly set you free if you embrace it.

In building your business, you are simply looking for people who are looking. If you are talking with someone who is in the middle of a move from one house to another, they probably will not be excited about joining your business. If they are dealing with an illness, ending a marriage, filing for bankruptcy, nursing an ailing parent, or in the midst of a lawsuit, the timing is likely to be challenging for them. Your job is to share your business and products with people every single day, but find people for whom the timing is perfect. Listen with your heart to everything they say, and believe them if they tell you the timing is off for them. If you listen with empathy and make it clear you have heard them, it is possible they will think of you in the future when their situation changes. You may be the only person who has listened to them for months. Share what you have, listen intently for what they say and what they don't say, and make good notes to which you can refer in the future. If someone has lost a spouse to death or divorce, they may be in deep sorrow as you talk with them. Months down the road, however, the timing could be just right for them to reconsider joining you and your business.

You may feel that your opportunity is perfect for a specific prospect, and you may be completely shocked when they do not see it the way you do. Practice nonattachment. Thank them for taking the time to sit down and listen. Ask them, "Who do you know who might be interested in staying at home with their kids, firing their boss, or starting their own business?" Being unattached will help them feel comfortable in referring a friend or colleague, and it will help you release any anxiety about seeing them in the future at the store or at a neighborhood barbecue.

A friend in my business once asked me, "Carrie, how are you able to stay detached from someone for whom you just know the opportunity is right, for whom you care so much, and who has said no to the opportunity? It is really hard for me not to be attached to them."

I really got what she was saying and acknowledged that it can be difficult. I told her, "You can stay attached to them; just don't be attached to their decision." This is a subtle, though important, distinction and one that will set you free. You can share from your heart and not feel pain when your friend or prospect opts out.

Let me make it even easier to grasp the concept of detachment. Consider the waitress at the coffee shop who is hustling from table to table, offering coffee. One, two, or even three customers may say, "No, thanks." A customer may even put his or her hand over the cup and say, "No way, not coffee. This is tea." The waitress does not storm away with hurt feelings and let it ruin her day. Her customer's "no" is not personal. He just doesn't want coffee right then and that's all. Undoubtedly there will be another customer who exclaims, "Yes, please. Where have you been? I'm looking forward to this cup of coffee."

I remember being at the park with one of my young boys, watching a soccer game. You know what that looks like. Two swarms running up and down the field, trying to put the ball into the net. I was distracted by a woman on my side of the field who was walking toward me and offering the contents of a brown paper bag to each parent on the sidelines. Every person looked into the bag and answered, "No, thank you." I was curious to know what everyone was saying no to. She got to my husband, Gordon, who glanced into the bag and practically shrieked, "No way—I hate avocados." I chuckled and asked her if I could take a look.

I eat an avocado nearly every single day in my salads, and they are expensive. These were perfectly ripe, right off her tree. I was *delighted*. I asked her if I could take a whole bunch, since so many people were turning them down. She was happy that I was so excited. She had not decided that her avocados were no good, even though tons of people had rejected them. She did not throw them away in the nearest trash bin and decide they were worthless. She just offered them to the next person on the field—*me*. I took as many as I could carry and smiled to myself. *This is just like building my business*, I thought as I walked to the car: *some will, some won't. So what? Someone's waiting.*

SHOWING THE PLAN— SIFTING AND SORTING

The goal in network marketing is to show the plan to two hundred new people and expect to sponsor twenty. You should sponsor one in ten, a 10 percent conversion rate. This formula is for the average network marketer just starting out, the person who has a full-time job and has limited time to invest in their business. By the way, if you want great results and are able to work the business full-time, you will become more effective faster and will likely have a much higher closing ratio.

Here is another one of my quirky analogies. Imagine you are holding a bag of two hundred M&M's. The bag contains yellow ones, red ones, green ones, brown ones and orange ones. Twenty blue M&M's are also in the bag. Your goal over the next few months or years—or however long it takes—is to go through this bag of two hundred M&M's and find the blue ones. These blue M&M's are your potential generals. You may find a blue M&M right away, or you may go through ten or twelve before you find your first blue one. You may find your blue M&M's toward the top of the bag, in the middle of the bag, or all clumped together at the bottom. When you pull out a green one, you do not get depressed, sad, or hurt. You certainly do not try to lick off the candy coating and make it blue. You just put it to the side and keep looking for the blue ones. You are not attached to the results, because you know there are twenty blue M&M's in the bag, and you are going to find them because you are committed and persistent, and have a strong work ethic. This is what you must do in network marketing. You are sifting and sorting, looking for people who want to build a business like you do. Your job is to share the details of your business every day with enthusiasm, passion, and confidence. Do this with zero attachment to the results. Your job is to ask questions, show the plan, follow up efficiently, really listen to people, help them get what they want, and track your numbers. The harder you work, the luckier you get.

So you have shown the plan to two hundred people using third-party validation, and you have enrolled twenty. Each of the twenty people has made an investment and told you they are joining to build a business. At this point, most of us would assume these distributors would run out and immediately share the products and business with their family, friends, and coworkers, right? Wrong! And this is the tough part for the motivated and committed enroller. Of these twenty people, approximately 75 percent will do nothing. Some will attend a meeting or two, and some will attend meetings for months. Some will learn the details about the products and business but never pick up the phone. Some will disappear without a trace, as if they have entered the witness protection program. You could take this personally and conclude that you are a terrible sponsor and must be doing something wrong. You are not. These are just the numbers. This is just the way it is. Let me explain further.

Of the twenty enrolled, fifteen have disappeared. You have five left. They enlist distributors and remain positive and coachable. They feed their minds with information from books and CDs. They conduct and attend weekly meetings in their homes or the homes of their distributors. Of these five, one person will be a "runner". This person will work diligently and will either call you all the time or never call, depending on his or her personality style and experience. You could not stop them if you tried. This is the "1-percenter".

As you learn more about your Company and its compensation plan, you will get a keen understanding of just how many leaders and runners you will need to reach the income goals you have set for yourself. If you have not met your goal after going through your first two hundred people, you will need to go through two hundred more. By all means, track your numbers. In this way you will undoubtedly see yourself becoming more effective. After a year, you may be enrolling two or three out of ten people instead of just one. You are likely to become more effective because competence breeds confidence. Whatever your numbers, you must practice the mantra, "I will until!"

SETTING EXPECTATIONS

As you develop your mind-set, I invite you to remember a few things. First, you are just sorting. Yes. No. Maybe. It's just like the M&M's. Greens over here, yellows over there, reds against the wall, browns beside the table, and blues follow me. Very few will say, "Yes, sign me up!" Don't start dreaming about retirement just because someone does react this way after hearing your opportunity presentation.

A "lay down" occasionally occurs in network marketing, just as it does in other businesses. Without hesitation, the potential customer says, "Yep, I'm in." In network marketing we refer to these folks as "jumpers". This happens rarely, and it can be a bit shocking. There are no questions or objections, just "Let's go!" It is very exciting, and by all means you should just go with it. A new network marketer might be so shocked and surprised that they continue to sell and tell, and fail to enroll their new prospect on the spot. Please do what they ask you to do and enlist them as a distributor in your business. Do not look shocked, confused, or overly delighted. Don't think, "*Yes, I've got one.*" Just do what they ask you to do. Enroll them, give them a quick orientation and homework (we will discuss this later), and move on. Also know that many times these jumpers end up doing nothing at all.

Once in a while you will enroll a runner. Runners identify

themselves by their actions and not their words. Like jumpers, runners sometimes surprise you, but in a more positive way. You will not identify them by what they say. You will know them only by what they do, and we all know that actions speak louder than words. The point is that whether you get a jumper, a runner, a new customer, or a "No, thank you," your actions are moving your business forward—all the time. Stay focused on action and unattached to results. Whatever happens, you have won. You are working! You are in full swing and moving in the direction of your dreams, no matter what anyone else does. Remember we are laying the foundation and developing a Venus mind-set.

In setting proper expectations, here are a few things to remember:

1. You are not out to *get* someone. You are looking for someone who is *looking*. If the M&M is blue, keep it and let go of the rest.
2. You are not *desperate*. You do not need any particular person. You are looking for someone who wants what you have.
3. You are a businessperson who has just started your own enterprise. You are the sole proprietor. You are the CEO of your own business. You are looking for people who want to create personal and financial freedom, just like you do.
4. Your business is strong when your mind is strong. Your business is weak when you are uncertain. If necessary,

fake it until you make it. Act as though failure is impossible, and it will be.

5. People do not join network marketing; they join you. Be the person you want to attract. Like attracts like. Emulate people whom you admire and become the entrepreneur with whom you would want to work.

6. Guard your dreams. Visit them every day (it helps to write them down too). Do not let anyone steal your dreams or your opportunity for free time and financial freedom.

7. Do not worry about the judgment of others. Do not make assumptions or take anything personally. If you are so inclined, pick up *The Four Agreements*, by Don Miguel Ruiz (1997). This book will help you detach from the opinions of others and take responsibility for your part in each encounter. Remember—other people are not paying your bills. You are. They have no voice in how you live your life. In fact, they probably spend little time contemplating what you are doing with your life, because they are too busy thinking about what they are doing with theirs. Stay on your side of the street. There is plenty of work to be done there.

8. Your business will never be bigger than you are. Grow yourself, and your business will expand.

Here's one more analogy before we move on. Have you ever watched a building go up in your community? We acquired a Target store in our neighborhood about two years ago, and we were all delighted when it started. A big sign was posted in the giant empty lot that read "Target—Coming Soon". We were ecstatic. I love Target! When the sign appeared, we all talked about it. "Did you see there is a new Target going up across from the sports field?" We speculated, "Do you think they will build a bridge, so that we can walk across the busy street while the kids are practicing?"

After a few months, the talk died down. We saw a few trucks and a handful of workers from time to time, but zero progress. It appeared the project had been abandoned. We stopped guesstimating about a date for the grand opening and continued to drive twenty minutes up the road to the Target in a neighboring town. We thought the city had changed its mind.

Time passed. An entire soccer season went by. Suddenly the site was jumping with activity. Workers appeared and two-by-fours and concrete blocks were dropped off. Framers came on the scene, and the building was erected in what seemed like a couple of weeks. A new sign appeared that said, "Target is now hiring." We were stunned at how fast it happened. It was exciting! We marveled at how organized and efficient the crew had been. It was our perception that Target was built with ease and grace; that it went up practically overnight. I can only imagine the reaction of the foreman and the crew had they been listening to our conversations. "Overnight? Not hardly, ladies and gentlemen."

I am sure they would have had an entirely different perspective. Consider what had to be done before the concrete foundation could even be poured. I am not an engineer, but I can surmise that leveling the ground, prepping the area for proper drainage, securing the electrical system, and creating a system for plumbing had to happen long before the building could ever take shape.

So it is with your network marketing enterprise. You will feel underpaid for months as you sift and sort through people, looking for the "generals" who will be interested in building an army with you. The no's will be plentiful, and you will learn how difficult it is to find "a few good men". Like the Target store, it may look like nothing is happening for a while. You may wonder if your business is ever really going to thrive!

GAINING MOMENTUM

Then one day someone who "gets it" will join your business. They will do what you do. They will take ownership of their organization and will bring in a friend or two. Their friend will bring in a friend or two, and you will be ecstatic. For a brief moment, you will be able to do the fun part—the training, motivating, and inspiring. Everyone loves doing this part, but just like the Target store, your business cannot go up without the laying of a firm foundation. If you continue to sift and sort and find your leaders, your business will eventually hit a tipping point. It will come together, and you will have to run like the wind to keep up. I have experienced this twice in my career, and I have watched countless others strap on their roller skates. You need to be ready to roll!

This is what I refer to as "personal momentum". It can be created any time you put massive action, effective execution, and time together in the same place at the same time. If you are lucky, and your personal momentum coincides with that of the company, you may experience the proverbial ride of your life. Remember that you must see it to achieve it. It is like a wave in the ocean. Get ready, get set—and paddle like heck to create your personal momentum. Grab that momentum to zip to the shore. My heart is racing just thinking about the rush!

Momentum: This is where preparedness meets opportunity. As Roy Spence, author of *It's Not What You Sell, It's What You Stand For* (2009), says, "Opportunity is the place where your talents and the needs of the world intersect." The needs of the world are obvious and plentiful. Network marketing could potentially be the answer for millions. Success is about making the leap and getting busy. This business is 10 percent inspiration and 90 percent perspiration. Get to work. The world is waiting for *you* to step up and step in. It's time for each of us to get off the sidelines and create something valuable and meaningful. Are you in? Before you shout yes, let me give you one final mind-set nugget.

With all the talk about waves, momentum, and the Target store, I've focused on up, up, *up!* Let me remind you of one last pitfall that can take you down, down, down. It's called procrastination, and it can stop you in your tracks. Most of us are notorious for "getting ready to get ready". Just like having kids or starting an exercise program, we often wait for that perfect moment that never really comes. We want to finish a project, clear some space, create some time, acquire more money, wait until work slows down, get healthier, or get rid of a spouse. Excuses are endless. You can add hundreds of them to this list. I delayed writing this book even when God gave me the most beautiful sign, a teeny rainbow in some puffy white clouds in the midst of a flight back to Orange County two years ago. If someone had asked me, "Carrie, do you consider yourself a procrastinator?" I would have responded without a blink. "I absolutely do *not*. No way, José, not me. I am a mover and shaker, baby. I take action. No grass is growing under my feet."

I have had to reconsider this belief. It is humbling to take a fearless moral inventory of yourself, but I encourage you to do it. Take a look inside, and ask, *"Am I taking action? Or am I making excuses and putting off until tomorrow what I could do today?"* Be open to examining your reasons for not getting started now. Are they valid, or are you scared? Is the timing right but you're terrified? Nobody can answer those questions but you. Take the time to do it. Take the time to reflect, assess, ask, and listen in silence. The answers are within you.

Get ready, get set. Let's do this thing. We will start from the beginning. You have just signed up. *Now* what do you do?

4

The Very Important First Forty-Eight Hours

Your "Why" and Your "What" Clearly Defined

HERE IS THE SCENARIO. YOU have just enrolled, and you are eager to begin building your business. Now what?

Your first assignment is to button your lip. That's right: keep quiet and do not talk. Just *zip it*! You are probably far too excited and too new to run out and share anything about your new business. In this profession, this is known as "ignorance on fire". As you walk in the door at nine o'clock on Tuesday night, after attending a meeting and then enrolling, you have probably reignited some of the heartfelt dreams that you held inside for years. You may be looking forward to sharing the news with your wife, husband, mother, or roommate. However, they may be ruminating about a problem at work, doing their taxes, or watching a game. In spite of your natural desire to share your enthusiasm, this may not be the time.

Instead, now is the time to guard and nurture your new business idea like you would a fledgling two-inch seedling that you just planted. Protect it from the wind, the rain, and the naysayers. When you walk in that door, your knees may be knocking as you experience contradictory feelings—excitement over what you have just committed to, and concern evoked by asking yourself, "*What in the world have I done?*" Being in touch with both internal doubts (head stuff) and excitement (heart stuff), you may be exuberant, passionate, and a little overwhelming to other people. Now is the time to take a breath and consider when will be the best time to share your new business with a partner, parent, child, spouse, or friend. Remember—they did *not* attend the meeting, meet your new business partners, or hear about the remarkable products, timing, Company, or income potential. You know much more than they do, but they are not likely to realize that. Keep it to yourself for now. The right time will present itself. Trust that you will know *exactly* when to talk about your wonderful new enterprise.

If you are a good student of network marketing, you have probably ordered and maybe even begun to read some of the books mentioned previously. Embarking on this learning path is imperative. You must *become* a network marketer. This may or may not happen on the day you sign up. There may be a clear distinction between the day you get into network marketing and the day it *gets into you*. You may not become aware of this distinction for months or even *years*. Eventually, however, you will know precisely when that shift happens.

After enrolling, ideally you have a remarkable and involved sponsor who is available most of the time, who is very successful in the profession, and who lives next door. Unfortunately, this is rarely the case. Imagine if I had said, "Ideally you have the perfect home with two perfect kids, the perfect career, perfect parents, perfect health, and tons of time, and you never have a problem." You would probably give a little chuckle, or a whooping laugh, and say something like "Yeah, *right*." Our experience tells us that this is not a perfect world.

Let me assure you. Most people do not have "rock star" sponsors with whom they always see eye to eye. Just remember God is for you. The universe is for you. You were born for greatness, and your situation is perfect for your growth and your journey. This is Venus talking. You have everything you need to shine in this business, but nobody said it was going to be easy. You may need to reach out, reach up past your sponsor, reach around, and reach inside to gather the support you need to build your dreams and your network marketing team. Remember—no excuses. Where there is a will, there is a way. You can do this thing. You are smart, you are committed, and you will make it happen!

Some people enroll in network marketing for the community, for fun, or because they want to support family or friends. These folks may or may not be truly interested in building a successful network marketing business. Assuming you are committed to building a sustainable business, you must really be in touch with your "why" and your "what". What do you want from your network marketing business? What is your desired payoff? Why are you doing this in the first place? Why would you spend the money, invest your time, and risk your reputation to build this business?

Before your mind wanders, let me tell you why I believe that it is so critically important to truly know and understand your "why" and your "what". People will disappoint you. They will not call you back. They may avoid you, lie to you, or stand you up for a coffee conversation or a meeting. People may sign up, invest their money, and then never return your call. I am being real with you. This is going to happen. It happens in every other business as well, but usually to a lesser extent, and it can feel more personal in network marketing. Remember our conversation about the barrier to entry? Once you start to talk about your business, it will seem that everyone has been in the profession at one time or another, and consequently they will seem disinterested in your opportunity. As I mentioned before, most people go to the gym, get their nails done, or forget they ever joined a network within days of signing up to build a business. Typically, the initial investment is low and people's insecurity is high. Though they may have started their business on fire with enthusiasm, the fire is easily extinguished with just a sprinkle of disappointment. The truth is that there is a lot of "No" and "No, thank you" in network marketing, which can easily be felt as disappointment or even failure. Even if they know the sting of failure does not always readily heal, people naturally shy away from things that hurt, and they leave their network marketing business behind. The reality is that people are going to let you down. At least, you are going to perceive that they have let you down. Since perception is reality for all of us, I feel it is wise to prepare you.

When a prospect recounts a disappointing experience with network marketing or "no-shows" you, and does not even give you a chance to share your business, it is critical that you have that "why" anchored in your heart and mind, to give you the confidence to persevere. Think of it as your safety net. You are walking a tight rope for the very first time. One misstep without a net and *you are toast*. You need insurance. Every bump, every "no", and every setback should take you straight to your "why".

It is impossible to overstate the importance of your "why". You must discover and articulate it. Write it down. Make it crystal clear in your mind and burn it into your heart. Why?- because you are going to need it. Trust me.

For a person new to the profession of network marketing, the concept of identifying your "why" may not be easily grasped. Most people spend way too little time developing a clear mental picture of what they really want to create in the future and why they want to create it. After all, many of us were taught to believe that it is self-centered and greedy to do so. Are we *allowed* to dream about the life we want?

A friend of mine recently shared a story of how his "why" became more accessible to him, and I believe his story might help you.

His mentor asked, "Jim, do you know what *your* responsibility is versus that of the universe?" (Wow, deep question. It sounds like

Venus might have been in the room.) My friend is a people pleaser, and he rambled on, using a ton of his Martian skills, weaving an answer full of esoteric and lofty words and ideas. After a couple of minutes, his mentor chuckled and said to him, "You really do not know, do you?"

Somewhat chagrined, my friend smiled in uncomfortable agreement. His mentor said in a most Venus way, "Your only responsibility is to know what it is that you desire and why. The how, when, where, and with whom is up to the universe." Wow, how awesome is that? Let me make this crystal clear. You take care of the "what" and the "why". God, the universe and source, will provide the rest—the "where, when, and how". It is that simple, and yet it takes strong, committed faith. It is simple, but not easy.

Dr. Tom Barrett, author and motivational speaker, shared something at an event I attended more than ten years ago. I have never forgotten it. He invited us to take out the pretend binoculars every morning and visualize the dream that gets us out of bed each day. He asked us to imagine, using all five senses, exactly how it would feel to realize our dream. He suggested that we take two or three minutes to experience this dream in our conscious minds. I'm inviting you to do the same.

Pause now and think about what you will enjoy as a result of building your network marketing business. If you want to stay home with your children, then feel yourself taking them to the park. Which park will you go to? What will you wear? Is it summer or autumn? Will you swing with them, or talk with another mom on the park bench while you watch your children squeal, run, and jump with delight? What will you pack in the snack bag? Where will you go after the park? Will you check out the zoo, or go home to nap or read a book while your kids rest? The more you engage in this vision, the better success you will have.

Maybe you are a businessperson on the road. You leave in the morning before sunrise and return home after the sun has long set. Maybe you are constantly on the road, dealing with traffic and airports, and you often wake up wondering what city you are in and why in the world this job sounded so good all those years ago. Maybe you are fed up, and you want to sleep in your own bed next to your spouse, whom you love, and near the kids, whom you rarely see. Maybe you dream of getting up, going to the gym at five thirty, and building your own dream, instead of being a cog in the wheel of someone else's dream machine.

Perhaps you are a single woman, tired of reporting to a boss who has little regard for your schedule since you are not going home to a family. Maybe everyone thinks you should get to work early and stay late, since you presumably do not have many responsibilities outside the office. Maybe you have trouble dating because work is so demanding, and you really never know where your job ends and your personal time begins. Maybe you hate dressing up every day, and you dream of wearing sweats, taking a yoga class, or going to the gym. Maybe you fancy doing a job that you love from late morning until well past dinnertime, from the comfort of your home.

Maybe you like to paint, dance, sing, or play an instrument, but your daily grind is all but killing your creative inner spark. If any of the above scenarios even remotely resembles your current reality, now is the time to throw caution to the wind and dream. See it, believe it, feel it, and create it in your mind. Do you realize that nothing has ever come to fruition without first having been imagined? Not a novel, a song, a painting, a studio, a ball field, or Disneyland: Nothing.

You have a blank canvas, so start painting. Use those binoculars to see the life you will create for yourself. It takes courage. It takes time. It takes thought. It is risky to go that deep and dredge up desires that have been dormant for years or even decades. Most people are too afraid to go down this path. Are you? Will you?

Let's return to Dr. Barrett and his mind-set development strategy. After you have used the binoculars and imagined all that you will create for yourself, you *must take the next step*. You will pull out your "magnifying glass" and decide what you must do right now to bring that vision to fruition. Do you need to get into the office and pick up the phone? Do you need to drive to the coffee shop and meet with your prospect? Do you need to go to the gym and commit to making a new friend? What must you do to move in the direction of all that you desire? I assure you that arranging your desktop, listening to another audiobook, or researching your product online is not going to make your dream a reality. Be fearless in assessing yourself. *Action, not activity, will move you toward success in network marketing.*

TAKE ACTION

Decisions are very important, but action is essential. If you are scared, take action. If you are questioning your skill, take action. If you are worried about what others will think, take action. You will be bad before you are good, and good before you are great. Nobody reaches their dreams without feeling the fear and doing it anyway. Action is the fuel by which your dreams are realized. Be fearless, take a risk, and become better, more resilient, and more confident.

Maybe you can work your business only part-time. No problem. Be organized, focused, and committed. I have seen people be more effective working their network marketing business part-time than they are working their "real job" full-time. It's all about envisioning what you want, and then executing and following through. It's about *taking action*.

GOALS

Before you take action, you need to set a few goals. Maybe this is the very first time you have been asked to actually set goals, rather than just talking about setting them. Again, goal setting is not usually part of your home or school curriculum. In fact, most people spend more time planning their vacations than they do their futures. Incredible, but true! Take time to check out this research about goals.

Why do 3 percent of Harvard MBAs make ten times as much as the other 97 percent combined? In his book *What They Don't*

Teach You at Harvard Business School (1984), Mark McCormack shares the details of a ten-year study conducted on Harvard MBA students starting in 1979. The students were asked, "Have you set clear, written goals for your future and made plans to accomplish them?" Only 3 percent of the graduates had written goals and plans; 13 percent had goals, but they were not in writing; and a whopping 84 percent had no specific goals at all.

In 1989 they were interviewed again. The findings, although somewhat predictable, were nonetheless astonishing. The 13 percent of the class who had had unwritten goals were earning, on average, twice as much as the 84 percent who had had no goals at all. What about the 3 percent who originally had clear, written goals? They were earning, on average, ten times as much as the other 97 percent combined.

What is the message? Taking the time to establish and write down your goals will definitely help you earn more money. But money is not everything in my world, and it does not necessarily equal success and happiness. Setting and achieving goals has given me more than money ever could. Proper goal setting did far more than just boost my paycheck; it is a potent tool that made my dreams a reality. Goal setting will boost your confidence and channel your energies in positive, creative, and constructive ways. Goal setting will get you up in the morning with a fire in your belly, and keep you focused when the "dream stealers" hit you hard. Setting and sharing written goals with your supportive friends, family, and team members can help you stay accountable and on point. It makes you an excellent model for duplication, which is one of the true essentials of network marketing, and it will provide encouragement, innovation, and motivation for you and the others you care about in your life.

There are people for whom writing goals down does not seem to be worth the effort. They claim, "I cannot write down my goals. I have too many. Besides, I do not have enough time to write them all down." If you do not have time to write down your goals, where will you find the time to accomplish them?

GOAL-SETTING STRATEGIES

You know you need them, but how in the world will you set them when this is all so new? Ideally you have an enroller who is involved and building a business that you desire to emulate. This is not always the case. Most of the time there is someone a few positions above you who is passionate about you and your success, even if they do not yet know you exist. Ask your enroller for the contact information of people above you (your upline) and reach up, up, up! Chances are good you can find someone who will open their arms to you. You can always contact your Company and ask to be connected with the distributors in your upline organization. If you are unable to find someone with whom to connect in your own group, I suggest you attend a corporate-sponsored meeting or function and make a friend. Reach out and introduce yourself to people sitting to your right and left. Find someone with whom you identify and exchange numbers. Other people in the room will be as eager to connect as you are. I promise. I know it is true.

One of my dearest friends is someone I met at a meeting more than twenty years ago, and she and I had completely different "genealogies". We floundered around in the beginning and made tons of mistakes. We cold-called, attended meetings together, and shared our dreams and desires. When I was down, she was up. When she was down, I was up. We had a partnership then, and we still do today. I was in her wedding, and she was at the birth of our first son, Iain. She went through another pregnancy with me, and I went through two more pregnancies with her. I watched her become the mother of three remarkable sons. You will make some of your best friends through this great profession of network marketing. Because we work as entrepreneurs from our homes, we have been present and available to our families and to each other. What a gift it is to set your own schedule and manage your own time. The freedom and choice that network marketing offer are worth fighting for.

Let's get back to *you* and goal setting. You do not need to do this alone. Work with your enroller (also known as your sponsor), up-line partner, or a new friend who is also in the business. With them you can set goals and develop a plan to get what you want. You will start by determining your long-term goals—two to five years down the road and maybe even further out. Where do you hope to be in five to seven years? You are just like a brand new freshman in college who dreams of what they will be doing after graduation. You are now clear on your "why", so focus on the steps (goals) that mark your progress toward achieving your "what". You can then break these bigger goals down by setting some shorter-term, one-year goals, followed by monthly, weekly, and daily goals. Your Company probably will have a training system with built-in basic goals or milestones. I must mention again that people in our profession frequently overestimate what can happen in their first year in network marketing and dramatically underestimate what can happen in two to five years. Developing a long-term vision and a plan of action to support your goals in each time frame is critical. It is important to remember that you can have a dream, but without a plan, you cannot have a dream come true.

How many contacts will you make in a day or a week? With how many people will you sit down in a month or a year? Results are directly tied to the action taken. If you take little action, you will see few results. If you take massive action and give it enough time, the results can be significant. Remember—you will be bad before you are good, and good before you are great. Nobody gets to skip the being-bad part. It is required. It is natural and it happens. How in the world will you become a humble and effective teacher if you do not experience being inexperienced? How will you be an empathetic and conscious leader of people if you do not know what it is like to be brand new and terrified? Your only assignment is to move in a forward direction and keep moving. Focusing on action, you will still fall, but at least you will fall forward.

I've been practicing Bikram yoga for fourteen years. It is the hot, smelly, 105-degree carpeted room where you twist yourself into twenty-six incredible postures in your underwear and sweat out the good, the bad, and the ugly. People who love it love it, and I am one of them. When I began in 2002, I had been playing tennis, teaching aerobics, and running nearly every day. My body was a tight mess. My first class was very, very difficult. After that, I did Bikram yoga every single day for a year. I was committed from day one, and it was anything but easy. I heard the instructors say again and again, "Just try the right way. You get all of the benefits as long you try the right way." They said it over and over, class after class, year after year. Now I will say it to you. Listen to your mentors, read the training material, follow your leaders, become a student of the profession, and like Bikram says, "Try the right way." Remember to be patient with yourself. They also told me at yoga, "You are looking for progress, not perfection." Venus would tell you to be gentle with yourself and others. Building a network marketing business is not a sprint. It's a marathon.

So now you have determined your "why". You have set some goals with the help of your sponsor, upline partner, or new friend. Most importantly, your goals have been documented. Let me take a moment here to tell you why it is important to write down your goals and share them with another human being.

Let's imagine that you have been sharing your products and business with friends and colleagues for a few weeks, and you are experiencing success. You are really eager to share this with your twin sister. She is more than a sister; she is your soul mate. She has just had her second baby and lives in another state. This is your very first opportunity to share your new business idea, and you are excited beyond words. So you share it. You are a little more nervous than usual because this one matters. You love your sister, she loves you, and you have done everything together for years. You finish sharing the story of how you found the products, the Company, and your business partners. You invite your sister to take a look. She is silent. She does not say anything for a full ten seconds. Then she exclaims, "Come on, Sis. You have got to be kidding me. You are not going to do a pyramid thing. Are you crazy?"

It feels as if she has taken a straight pin to your shiny pink balloon. BAM! The air is all gone. You hardly remember the rest of the short conversation, as she mumbles something about getting the kids down for a nap and ends the call abruptly.

You are shaken. You are sad, irritated, frustrated, disappointed, and possibly quite angry. It's time to go to Venus. Take a breath and exhale completely. Close your eyes and pick up the beautiful piece of stationery where you wrote out your "why". Hold it near your heart and remember that your dream is real and you deserve it. See yourself living the life you have imagined. Breathe in—do it—and breathe out ten times, and forgive your sister for not understanding how important this is to you. Give her the grace that you wish she had been able to give to you. Now open your eyes and read your "why" with power and conviction. Read it again and more *loudly* this time. Read it one more time with everything you have, and remember that no one person matters in network marketing. You have no idea who is going to join you on your journey. It is not for you to decide. Your only job is to share it again and again. After you are calm and clear, pick up the phone and call your sponsor, partner, or friend. Share the experience and read your "why" one last time. Then get back to work!

Without delay, call the next person on your list. The next time you get shot down, it will hurt less and *you will be more*. They may knock you down, but you get up, brush yourself off, fuel your fire with your desires, and then go again. Just like the biker who takes a bad spill, the musician who forgets her notes, the comedian who gets no laughs, the cowboy who gets bucked off the bull, or the attorney who loses the case. You are the boxer who just received a left hook; no more, no less—no crying, no feeling sorry for yourself. You have places to go, people to help, dreams to fulfill, and a business to build. Don't allow anyone to steal your dream.

If you have a sponsor and/or a friend with whom you are working, you have a business relationship. You will be locking arms and walking (or running) together. The pace will be up to you. The point is, you need not do this alone unless that is your choice. There is always someone, somewhere (even outside your state) with whom to partner. The sooner you sponsor that first person locally, the sooner you have a friend with whom to work right in your area. This is why it is so important to sponsor people whom you enjoy. I often tell people, "The reason I am so passionate about having you join me in my business is that I like you. If you get in, we are going to spend more time together."

It is important that you respect the people you invite to look at your business. We often say, "No mean people." Do not share your business with anyone with whom you do not want to travel the world. If you sponsor them, it is your responsibility and duty to teach, guide, and care about them. If you have been the product of a drive-by sponsorship, then find someone you respect, someone to whom you can relate in the business and with whom you can work side by side. Do your goals together, exchange your "whys", and lift each other up. Nobody wants to work in a void. Everyone wants to be part of something bigger than him or her. Find someone you love to be around and do this business together!

5

ON LEADERSHIP AND DEVELOPING LEADERS

I WANT TO SHARE SOMETHING that has helped me in building my own network marketing business and in understanding how to inspire and develop other leaders along the way. It is not too early to mention that *you are only as successful as the leaders you develop.* This piece is pivotal. Bear this in mind while I share an experience.

Many years ago, I took a training called Landmark Education. Although I learned many remarkable things in that training, one concept has been exceptionally beneficial in my business endeavors as well as in this journey called life. The instructor drew a circle on the chalkboard and sectioned off a small piece of this pie. He said, "This represents what you know that you *know*." Then he sectioned off another piece of the pie and said, "This is the piece that you know that you *don't know*." Then he showed us the biggest part of the pie and changed my thinking forever when he said, "This is the piece that you *don't know that you don't know.*" I did not know then what I do know today, which is this: The piece that *you don't know that you don't know* becomes more important the older you get and the more you learn. In network marketing, this piece can derail you and your new people.

When you get into network marketing, you are excited. You will hear that a former dishwasher is making thousands of dollars per month. You will meet truck drivers, fitness instructors, housewives, underground miners, dental assistants, and waitresses who have transformed their lives and their moneymaking abilities, and those abilities are now on display to inspire the masses. These people have become great students, followed the leaders, developed their strengths and talents, and reached the top ranks of their respective companies. When prospects are exposed to these people or their stories, they tend to become extremely optimistic about their *own* potential success. Please note, however, that it is often easier for these everyday folks to dig in, take action, and check their egos at the door than it is for your typical doctor, lawyer, or corporate executive. Tons of education can be a bit of a stumbling block in our profession, because a highly educated person tends to question *everything.* They often spend time in "analysis paralysis" and their egos often keep them from acknowledging what they don't know. Subsequently they often have trouble getting traction.

CONSCIOUS COMPETENCE LADDER

Here is the piece that you will need to internalize and share with the other people who join your business. Called the Conscious Competence Ladder, this is another segment of the pie I didn't know that I didn't know. I *do* know it now and you will too. It is something you can take with you for the rest of your life. Noel Burch, an employee of Gordon Training International, developed it in the 1970s. She created this concept to help people gain a clearer understanding of the various stages a person goes through in learning a new skill. If you have a keen understanding of these stages, you can keep a new person in the network marketing business long enough to achieve some success.

When a new person joins network marketing, they tend to want to share their new business immediately. And with whom do they want to share it? You've got it: they share it with those people who are closest to them, the people who matter to them the most. If you saw a good movie, read a great book, or ate at a fantastic restaurant, you would not stop a stranger on the street or purchase a prospect list to share your excitement, right? Of course not! You would want a friend, parent, coworker, or family member to experience just what you did. Why? Because you care about them, respect them, love them, and want them to experience the best things in life.

The biggest problem I see in network marketing today is that a new person hits the fear-of-failure wall and cannot see past it to the light at the end of the tunnel. What initially appeared easy can seem impossible within a matter of days, if a person is hit hard with rejection right out of the gate. However, if a new person is trained in the details of the Conscious Competence Ladder, he or she will *expect* to feel ineffective and slightly lost in the beginning, and he or she will know that this feeling is part of the learning process.

At level one, the bottom rung of the ladder, you are an unconscious incompetent. You don't know that you don't know all there is to know about your endeavor. You do not have sufficient skills or knowledge about network marketing. Here is the part that gets people. You do not even know you are unskilled, so your expectations and confidence level may be much higher than they should be. This often coincides with "ignorance on fire" and sets you up to get shot down when you least expect it.

After a few weeks, a few days, or even a few minutes, you recognize your lack of skills and become a conscious incompetent. Unless you have beginner's luck and hit success right away, you become completely aware of how ineffective you are. Your confidence is gone and sometimes so are you. You are beginning to know what you don't know, whereas people around you seem to be confident and comfortable. Everyone except you seems to know exactly what they are doing. In your mind, the waitress and the underground miner are smiling and enjoying huge success, but you are not. You are freaked out, and you decide network marketing is not for you. Since your investment is relatively low and you have a lot of products, it is not too hard to walk away, which is what many people choose to do.

Let's pretend you are a brand new franchise owner attending

a weeklong training in another state. You are likely to feel over-whelmed and unskilled. You are a conscious incompetent. But here is the difference. With the franchise, you have made a huge financial investment. Your commitment level is much higher. You have skin in the game. You have far more to lose and are not so quick to walk away, because you expect this discomfort, and you are confident that you can navigate the learning curve, the fear, and the confusion. As you can see, this is where we lose most new people in network marketing. This is also why helping them set a realistic timeline and expectations will help to mitigate some of the feelings of fear and inadequacy they are likely to feel in this stage of learning. This is the Venus way of doing business. Do not over-promise or under deliver at this stage, or it will be a deal breaker for your new enrollee.

With realistic expectations, strong commitment, and good coaching and support, you are likely to reach level three of the Conscious Competence Ladder and become a conscious compe-tent. You are learning how to share the products and business with others. You are gaining skills and confidence in putting them into practice. You have learned the lingo and are familiar with network marketing jargon. It does not yet flow easily off your tongue, but you now know what you are doing and gain confidence every time you do it. In other words, you know that you know. You are earn-ing as you are learning, and your actions become more natural. If you spend enough time in this stage, you are sure to reach level four and become an *unconscious competent*. This is where the business becomes really fun.

Level four of the Conscious Competence Ladder is the place where everything simply flows. You are confident about what you have to offer, and you absolutely *know* that it is not for everyone. The best part is that you are completely unattached to the outcome of every single interaction. You do what you do every day with excitement in your heart. You offer your products and business because it is difficult *not to do so*. Sharing what you have is part of who you are now. If people share their problems and you have potential solutions, you feel a loss if you *do not share*. Your skills have become habits, and you talk to people with ease and grace. You do not even know that you know. It is easy for you now. People are drawn to you because you are becoming the leader they want to be. It is at this point that you want to help as many people as possible to get past the first three stages. Strong leadership is what takes a company from good to great!

OVERCOMING FEARS AND BEING OPEN AND WILLING

Now that you are a couple of days, weeks, or months into your network marketing business, it is time to become consistent and patient. You have learned. You have stretched yourself and grown. You have taken some hard knocks, and you *deserve* a win if you have not achieved a few already. You are being tested. You are developing your mental muscles. God is preparing you for more, and you can ask for divine guidance every day. In silence, ask, "Where do You want me to go? What do You want me to do? What do

You want me to say? To whom?" In this way, your lessons will be brought to you. As you say yes to that quiet inner voice, you will move closer and closer to the dreams you are envisioning for yourself and your loved ones. This is the *truth*!

In your movement up the Conscious Competence Ladder, remember that nobody is good at everything, and be aware of the rung on which you are standing. For example, after years as a family therapist, you may be an excellent communicator and find that problem solving comes naturally to you. You may be an *un*conscious competent in this area. You do what you do because it is easy, and it is second nature to you. Conversely, you may be very apprehensive when picking up the phone to invite a friend to take a look at your products and business. You may feel like a conscious incompetent in this arena. It is important to recognize where you shine in your business and where you do not yet. Be realistic about where you are, so that you'll become inspired to partner with someone else to get where you would like to be.

There is another reason you need to know which rung of the Conscious Competence Ladder on which you stand, and this is critical. If you know where you are in the learning process, you can be of better help to the people who are joining your business.

If you are low on the ladder with regard to prospecting, you may unconsciously project your fear onto your new person. You may be very nervous and keep warning her about all the things that can and will go wrong. You may be working with a self-confident person who, unlike you, has *no* problem picking up the phone to call a prospective business partner. Be careful to allow them the freedom to run their business without interference from your issues.

I see a parallel in child rearing. It has been easy for me to project my fear onto our teenage boys. Our sons are very different from each other and from me. Our younger son Cameron has self-confidence of which Iain and I could only dream. Cam's attitude is "Like me or don't like me. It makes absolutely no difference to me. I am who I am and I like myself." I finally adopted this philosophy at age fifty. (What's the rush?) Warning Cam about how cruel and fickle kids can be would have been projecting my issue onto him.

Conversely, our elder son, Iain, is laid-back and easygoing about competition. He is gifted at everything he tries—basketball, soccer, violin, drums, ping-pong, pool, and skateboarding, to name just a few—but he could not care less about winning. I used to remind him that it was all about having fun and that he should not stress himself out about performing and excelling. Looking back now, I think it is funny. Iain would be out on the soccer field picking flowers and examining them. He would be facing the wrong way for kickoff, checking out the neighboring game, or dreaming about where he would go after the game. Iain spent little time worrying about the outcome. The last thing on his mind was winning or losing. My worries about his fragile ego and his developing psyche were mine. They were unwarranted and unfounded.

Allow me to give you a real-life example of how one person's fear can infiltrate the network marketing tribe.

I remember when a new distributor was extremely apprehensive about offering the full enrollment package available through her network marketing Company. Her opinion was that it was too expensive and that nobody could afford it. She told me again and again that her people did not have the money and could not possibly make such a big investment. (By the way, it was less than $1,000.) It was clear to me that she was projecting these thoughts onto her potential business partners. Because *she* was struggling financially, she presumed everyone *else* was struggling. She offered the package and immediately helped them decide that a lesser option made more sense. Not surprisingly, they jumped at the lesser option. I pointed out to her that she had a "lack" mentality. I assured her that some of her people would conclude that the package was well priced and highly accessible to them. She was unaware that she was leading her people to make a buying decision with which *she* was more comfortable. Once she changed her behavior, people signed up for the full enrollment package without hesitation. Remember—thoughts become things, whether you are building a business or parenting your children. You must tend to and weed out those six inches of real estate between your ears. Pull out the thoughts that do not serve you, your children, and your potential business partners. Remember your people come with history. They had a life before network marketing and undoubtedly gathered some skills there. Skills *transfer*.

Let's look at another scenario. You may be an excellent presenter and have little or no fear of being in front of the room. Perhaps you have been a teacher or a life coach, and public speaking is comfortable for you. You are an *unconscious competent* in this regard. It will be critical to remember that most people are very nervous about getting up in front of the room. Although I believe that we all can *learn* to present, most of us have not yet developed the skill. You will need to communicate fully and ask good questions to determine where people stand on the Conscious Competence Ladder and how open they are to coaching. In fact, you will need to assess where you are and how open you are to guidance and suggestions as well.

My advice is to be open. Be willing. Be generous. Be gracious. Be grateful, and do not take anything personally. People are generally good and kind with good intentions. Trust that everyone who has come into your life has something to teach you. Venus is begging us all to remember that we are here to lift each other up not to tear each other down. Because we are in network marketing where there are no bosses, few rules, and virtually no penalties for stepping on each other's toes, we must self-regulate and become radically accountable. Step outside yourself and be objective with regard to your skills and talents and with those of others. It will serve you. In this way, we will elevate network marketing for all to enjoy.

6

ONCE STARTED, SOME THINGS **NOT** TO DO

SINCE MANY PEOPLE WHO JOIN network marketing have either never tried it, tried it without success, or are just nervous about what to do next, it might be helpful to share some insights about what to avoid doing in your network marketing journey.

I laugh at myself while remembering my early parenting. Saying "no" or "not" was a full-time job for me when my kids were little. "Do not hit your brother." "Do not spit anywhere but the bathroom." "Do not leave the cap off the toothpaste." "Do not leave the toilet seat up." "Do not touch the hot iron." "Do not get out of the car on the street side." "Do not stick your gum on the underside of the table." "Do not put your dirty fingers in your mouth." When my boys were three and five years old, my doctor coached me: "Do not say "no" too much. Find ways to say "yes".

In network marketing, as in parenting, we must choose our

battles in guiding and coaching our business partners. Nobody wants to be nagged about *not* doing this and *not* doing that. There are gentle ways to make suggestions. The Venus way of building this business is firm, but kind and forgiving. Give guidance, or accept it from your sponsor, but then step away and allow this new person to learn by natural consequences. We are in business *for ourselves* but not *by ourselves*. Some people want to grit it out and learn by making their own mistakes. Some want tons of input and coaching; either way is right. Assessing your personal preference and that of your people will be critical to your success.

ABOUT CONTROLLING YOUR ENTHUSIASM

It is not uncommon for people to get really excited and come up with lots of creative ideas when they first join network marketing. They want to take tons of shortcuts to reach as many of their contacts as possible as fast as possible. This is a Mars way of thinking: "Get out of my way. I'm going to go out and sponsor everyone!"

I am reminded of a wonderfully talented and influential doctor who joined my business a few years ago. The night he became a distributor, he could not sleep. We were scheduled to meet the following morning, but he just couldn't wait. He was so excited about the products and business that he got up in the middle of the night and crafted an incredible e-mail sharing the details of his new business with three thousand contacts. I certainly understood his enthusiasm, but I hope I do not have to tell you this is not the most efficient way to start out. Do you think anyone feels special when they receive a mass e-mail from a credible friend or colleague who has become a passionate network marketer? My grandpa would have said that my doctor friend went off "half cocked," and I have to agree. I believe it goes back to that low initial investment and the fact that nearly anyone can try their hand at network marketing. If that same doctor purchased an expensive franchise today, I sincerely doubt he would open his doors for business tomorrow. A little bit of preparation and planning goes a long way in our business.

Many people try to reinvent the wheel when they get into network marketing. They are especially drawn to ideas that excuse them from having to contact people whom they know personally. Often a new distributor will tell me about the opportunity to share their products at a neighborhood flea market, the booth at the local PTA meeting, or the table at the church bazaar. I cannot help but conclude that they are uncomfortable with the thought of calling a friend or family member to share their new business. Often they say something like "I'll contact my brother later when I am making money" or "I would rather talk with strangers until I get good at this." If you feel this way, you are not alone. The fear of being rejected by a close friend or coworker is real. Getting shut down by a stranger seems far less painful. After years of watching people try these tactics, I will tell you without hesitation that they rarely work. It is often expensive, always time consuming, and generally ineffective to pursue people who you do not know personally. People join people they know and trust.

Remember—you must be inviting people to join your business. If you have a booth at the fair at which you're creating awareness and brand recognition for your Company but not enrolling people, you are wasting your time. People might listen with interest and even respond enthusiastically. They will admire your display and pick up your brochure. They may even visit your website. But they are not likely to give you their credit card and join as a new business partner. They do not know you or trust you—and why should they?

Sometime down the road, a friend or business associate will approach that same person with the same information. They will remember that they saw it somewhere previously and were moderately interested. They will be more open-minded now, and they might even join right on the spot. Their first exposure to the business was through *you*, but they are more likely to sign up with their mother, business associate, or friend. *You* did the groundwork and they read *your* brochure. *You* piqued their interest, but they joined with someone else. People generally do business with people they *know and trust.*

ABOUT "SELLING" THE PRODUCT

Here is another thing to consider about the new person's reluctance to reach out to the people about whom they care the most. A new person will try to sell their products, which can be extremely uncomfortable no matter how much they believe in them. Although it is true that everyone likes to buy, no one likes to be sold to. I remind people every day that I do not sell products. If someone needs my products and tells me so, I will share them, and I always drop a hint about how they could potentially earn money. "If you become passionate about these products, I can help you create some residual income." I show people how to have more freedom, income, and choice. I teach people how to have more fun, travel, and enjoy a better lifestyle. I show them how to add more excitement, friendship, and personal development to their lives. I find out what people are missing, and try to meet their needs and satisfy their desires.

So what is the takeaway? The bottom line is to remember what you are offering and offer it with passion, conviction, and the sincere desire to be of service. If you can do that, you will be proud of who you are and what you do. You will be delighted to report, "I am a professional network marketer."

Do build your business with people whom you know and people who know you. There is no substitute for person-to-person, face-to-face, and heart-to-heart connection. It is best to meet your prospect personally to find out what is going on with him or her. Your friends and family will be far more likely to discuss something of concern to them if you are talking face-to-face. You will be more likely to figure out together whether what you have to offer may help them. Body language and facial expressions can tell you a lot about what a person is thinking and feeling. Meeting people in person is definitely to your advantage.

ABOUT MEETING PLACES

I want to share one more thing here. I recommend meeting prospects somewhere away from their world. Meeting at their home or office is not usually the best choice. Ideally you want to choose a place where you can have a good conversation with the fewest interruptions. Choosing a coffee shop near their home or workplace will typically allow for a better conversation and fewer distractions. I do *not* recommend scheduling lunch with a potential business partner. The greeting, order-taking, food-delivery, and check-paying processes can be disruptive and poorly timed when sharing your products and business for the first time.

7

WEBSITES, BUSINESS CARDS, AND SUPPORT TOOLS

COMPARED WITH OTHER BUSINESSES, LITTLE preparation is required to begin building your network marketing business. Learning a bit about the profession and some details about your Company and products, coupled with an understanding of the power of a winning mind-set, are enough to get you started. Clarifying your why and setting some goals will ignite your passion to move forward. You will need just a few additional things as support tools, although you don't need to wait for their arrival before making your first calls. If you do not start working your business right away, your new people will not start either. They will watch every move you make and follow suit. Your sponsor, upline partner, or sideline friend (someone that is not in your personal line of sponsorship) will be happy to provide you with the few things you need in the very beginning. In fact, most of what you need will be available to you online.

Most people are excited to order business cards, which make them feel more professional, but this is a personal preference. I have been in the profession for years, and I rarely use business cards. I build my business wherever I am, whatever I am doing. For years I have been a mom building my business in the nooks and crannies of my life. It has always felt a bit contrived when I produce a business card. Instead, I carry a very small spiral notebook and a pen in my purse. In chatting with a friend or a new prospect, I will usually say something like "Hang on a minute. Let me see if I can find something to write with and on so I can reach out to you." It sounds nonthreatening and casual. This relaxed approach tends to defuse the resistance that often arises when people correlate a business card with "Uh oh, here comes a sales pitch." This approach also increases the chances that you will have another conversation with them at a time and place more conducive to sharing your opportunity.

If you are comfortable using business cards, then by all means order some. I definitely suggest a card that does not have a company name or website on it. I would not want anyone to go to my network marketing website without first having a quick conversation with me. Remember—people are buying you. If you send them directly to your Company's website, they will make a snap judgment based on what they see. They usually will not spend more than a minute or so and may throw the proverbial baby out with the bathwater. If I get the chance to talk with them first, I can probe a bit and possibly hit on something that will pique their interest enough to motivate them to spend a little time on my site.

Your business card might say something like "ABC Marketing" or "Jim Dunton and Associates," or it might have the name of your small business. My business card says, "Carrie Dickie, Dickie Clan, Inc.," with "Leadership Development" underneath. My photo is on the front (I am hoping they remember me because they are buying me) along with my phone number and e-mail address. I rarely share this card, but have it in case I meet someone for whom a business card is important. Having a generic card allows you to remain in control of the flow of information and then follow up. If you just throw your business cards out there, you'll probably never hear back from anyone. Most people are busy and disorganized, and do not follow through. I do not ever want to lose a "hot one" because I gave up control of the connection process.

Having tools such as a DVD, brochure, or sample is another way of stimulating your prospect's curiosity. Sharing a few details and getting an e-mail address and cell phone number increase your chance of a second contact. If you pique someone's interest, give them a few details, exchange contact info, and then walk away, you remain in control. In contrast, if you just share your business card and a brochure, you have almost eliminated any possibility of a follow-up contact. The friend or colleague who gets a typical business card thinks that they have everything they need to make an informed decision, which is not true. Actually they have only what they need to make a snap decision and that decision is usually not a yes.

You may ask, "When in the world should I use tools and business cards if not when I meet someone for the first time?" That is a great question. Use a business card *after* you have sat together and talked about your Company and products. You will need a "leave-behind" tool such as a brochure, CD, or web address. These tools provide a third exposure. The first exposure is when you meet initially, and the second exposure is when you contact them for a sit-down appointment or invite them to attend an opportunity meeting. This third exposure (the brochure or website) occurs at their leisure, when they are likely to be more open to new ideas. You have shared what you have and formed a connection, and now they see that the ball is in their court. Follow up based on their level of interest and on what the two of you have mutually decided. Nowadays, with so much of our research being done online, sharing information about your business doesn't need to be expensive.

Again, network marketing is a simple business, but it is not easy. Comfort in meeting new people and reconnecting with previous acquaintances is a required skill. Practice makes perfect, and the more you do it, the better you get.

I want to share another helpful perspective with you before leaving this conversation. I remember when my friend and business partner was taken aback by something that caught his attention when we were talking one day about making connections out in the world. I said, "I don't go out to do network marketing. I just go out." Every morning I ask for guidance. "Who needs me today, God? Bring me people who are frustrated. Bring me people who are broke. Bring me people who are ready to change their lives. Bring me people who want what I have." Then I go to the gym, the bank, the grocery store, the car wash, and the post office. I am always prepared and ready to share what I have. My business is part of me now. I do it, because I cannot *not* do it. This is the vision of Venus. This is how Venus moves in the cosmos.

8

OVERVIEW OF THE PROCESS

SETTING YOUR INTENTION

AS IN ANY OTHER PART of your life, setting your intention is vital to the health and success of your business. Earlier we talked about clarifying your goals and your "why". Intention is an even deeper concept and referred to far more frequently on Venus. Using parts of the definition of *intend* I found on www.dictionary. com that resonates with the way I see it, I found "verb; c.1300; from Old French entendre, intendere—to direct one's attention (in Modern French principally 'to hear'), from Latin intendere— to literally stretch out, extend, from in- toward." To paraphrase, intend means to direct one's attention to, to stretch out, to extend from inside oneself toward, to hear." Perfect! That is just what I intended to present to you regarding intention.

As I read Caroline Myss, who referenced a work by author Jane Trahey, the Venus concept of intention became clearer to me. My interpretation was, "We each have a destiny that's been laid out for us. If we follow the intuitive prompts or the proverbial 'bread crumbs,' we will live it out. If we choose to ignore the lessons God has planned for us, we leave our journey to fate. By ignoring, we choose to flounder." While pondering the concept of destiny versus fate, I was prompted to Elton John's song "Candle in the Wind". In my estimation, living like a candle in the wind, off course and without intention, would be scary and unacceptable. No matter who you are or what you believe, I am certain that setting an intention each day will serve you.

In addition to assuring that I am on course, setting an intention each day reminds me that I am part of something bigger; that there is a master plan. In the morning, before I make my very first call, I ask for divine guidance. When I sincerely intend to enrich the lives of others and to live on purpose, my day unfolds by design. It is not my intention to be corny here. This is a truth for me, and I am passionate about it.

People tell me they are nervous about making calls and do not want anyone to think they are trying to "make money off of them". If you are having these feelings, it is because you are focused on yourself and not on the people whom you are calling. You are focused on what they will think about you and how they might judge you. In contrast, when you set your intention every day to focus on others, you will feel connected and empowered to act with confidence and conviction.

Let's focus on the business at hand. Now that we have spoken about the power of intention, it is time to make your prospect list. Who do you want to bless? Who do you want to prosper? With whom would you like to travel the world? Whose life would you like to change? Do not prejudge or analyze. Just write. If someone comes to mind, there is a reason. Perhaps it's because they are going to respond negatively to your business offer, which will toughen you up or strengthen your resolve. Maybe they are going to remind you about what Jane Trahey suggests: that turning your back on your destiny will leave your life to fate. Just remember that everyone has something to teach you. If you are teachable, think of your prospects in this way, and then you will be excited to write their names down. You will know that each one has a nugget of wisdom to share with you.

Tell yourself, *I am so lucky. I am on my journey. I am living on purpose. I am here by design, and each person I meet is by divine appointment.* Wow. This is powerful stuff. With this in mind, you will create a great prospect list.

BUILDING A LIST

On Venus, making the list is fun. You are never alone if you "plug in" before you start. Get quiet and ask for guidance. "Bring me the broke, the people in transition, the people you want me to serve." Again, this is really fun if your intention is strong. Do not worry about last names or even phone numbers. You can write names such as "Sherry from the yogurt shop," "Jim from the cleaners," or "Jen from school". Jot down phone numbers only when they are not in your phone. This can be a fast off-the-top-of-your-head process. Do not talk to yourself: *"Hmm, I'm not sure whether Sherry from the yogurt shop would be more interested in the product or the business; or Jim from the cleaners probably makes a ton of money already, and he is so busy. When would he ever find the time to make phone calls with his business and three kids?"* Do not analyze or judge. Try not to have a preconceived idea about each prospect's level of interest or potential involvement. Be open like a child: *Everyone is going to want to join me. Why wouldn't they? I'm having a blast, and they will want to do this too.* After a no, proceed with the innocence of a little boy or girl. *Oh well, I have another friend who will want to come out and play with me. I have tons of friends.*

Your cell phone is an excellent place to start. Do not cherry-pick. If their names are in your phone, write them down. Who does not deserve to choose the opportunity for free time and residual income? Who will not be given the opportunity to tell you no? Who will not have the chance to reject you and build your mental muscles? Again, everyone you know is here to teach you something if they end up on your list. Maybe you'll try to call them four times but they still won't return your call, and you will learn how uncomfortable rejection feels. How will you be an excellent leader and teacher for others if you have never experienced the sting of being ignored? How will you ever learn that it is not personal until you receive a phone call telling you that a prospect has just received a difficult diagnosis or divorce papers? These lessons are either learned voluntarily, which is much easier, or you will get them another day in another way that may not be as gentle. Be excited and willing to learn from every contact you make. You can even make notes next to each prospect's name as you contact them, documenting what you learned from them. Network marketing is challenging and *fun*.

I want to share a book that has affected my business and my life: *The Four Agreements* by Don Miguel Ruiz (1997). I have not mastered these agreements, but I have memorized them. I refer to them regularly, and they have helped me become a better person. You will have a richer experience calling your list of prospects if you have read this book. Do not wait to start calling, though. Order the book and pick up the phone. I will share two of the agreements with you to "nurture" you until your own book arrives:

Do not make assumptions.

Do not take anything personally.

Imagine. Making *any* call to *anyone* will not be a problem if you internalize these two agreements.

You will not sail through your list without feelings. You will be bad before you are good, and good before you are great. You will get better and more resilient as you go. You may feel that first no in your gut. You will wince when the first person asks you, "You are going to do what? Is that a pyramid scheme?" You may get easily bumped off course in the very beginning, but you will get more proficient, stronger, more committed, and less wobbly as long as you remain in action and moving forward. I am reminded of something that I heard at a lecture a few years ago. One of my mentors, the famous author and speaker Marianne Williamson, said, "I am not depressed by the gap that still exists between Jesus and me because I am so impressed by the gap that exists between Jesus and the me I used to be." I found that to be one of the wittiest and most authentic comments I have ever heard. Remember—in moving through your list of contacts, you are looking for progress, not perfection. Be patient and gentle with yourself. By treating yourself with kindness, you will likely be more kind and understanding with your brand new distributor down the road.

People often suggest a list of one hundred to two hundred names as a great starting point in building your business, but I believe the list should be longer. Shoot for five hundred to a thousand names. Remember we are not talking only about close friends and relatives. We are including everyone with whom you have come in contact in your lifetime that you can still find, and this is getting easier and easier with social media.

SHORT LIST VERSUS LONG LIST

Here is my philosophy on starting with a short list versus a nice, long, full one. Let's say you have one hundred names and then get together with your sponsor to make your very first calls. You dial through your list and leave about ten messages. You say something like "Jean, it's Carrie Dickie, and I am excited! Where are you? I have come upon something you just have to see! When the phone was ringing just now, I was saying, 'Answer, answer, answer,' but you didn't! You have *got to* call me right away!" After leaving ten messages, you are a little frustrated and perhaps a bit deflated. You cannot help but hear your internal dialogue: *Gosh, I have already called ten people and I only have ninety left!*

So, you speak to two friends personally. You go through the process of sharing your story, inviting them to an opportunity presentation, or asking them to take a look at a Company video. They are polite and tell you no. The time is not right for them and they are *off the list*. You have left ten messages and received two rejections, and it's abundantly clear that you have already made initial contact with 12 percent of your list! Your subconscious inner committee may be quite brutal when it taunts you: *Wow, we could potentially get through this list by tomorrow! Where will we go from here? We are definitely going to fail. It's time to quit!* That negative committee can be quite loud and convincing in the beginning. A list of five hundred will keep the committee quieter longer. It will build your confidence and infuse you with optimism. Anyone can come up with five hundred names with a little help from a friend. Your sponsor, upline, or sideline friend can be tremendously helpful in jogging your memory.

I remember when I first started out in direct selling many, many years ago. I asked a girlfriend to have a party for me and invite some friends over to take a look at my home décor items. I had just joined my Company, and their products were beautiful. I knew that my girlfriend and her friends would be interested in purchasing these products, since we were all young women raising kids, who wanted to beautify the homes in which we were spending so much time. I told her that she would receive "hostess dollars" and could earn some of these items simply for hosting the event. She was a yes until it came time to write the names down. She said, "I don't know anyone, Carrie. I really don't have that many people to invite." I took out the little notebook I carry in my purse and said, "You can start by inviting your two sisters, right?" She agreed, and I wrote down their names. Then I reminded her about the women on our tennis team and added them to the list. I recalled names of friends about whom she had spoken in the past, and the list was soon more than thirty names. She started to get excited and began to add to the list without prompting. I had her call each person individually. She left exciting messages, full of enthusiasm, asking them to call her back. When we had the party two weeks later, fifteen women attended, they all bought my products, and my friend got beautiful things for her home at no cost!

So here is the takeaway. I started writing the list, not her. I got out my pen and notebook and started jogging her memory. I was writing and she was lifting her gaze, thinking of people she could invite. I shared details about what she stood to gain and then built a bridge from her resistance to her full engagement in the process. This is what your network marketing partner can do for you, and what you will do for *your* new people when the time comes. Projects are more enjoyable when you are working with a friend. This is what makes network marketing so much fun!

HOW TO BUILD YOUR LIST

An opportunity meeting is different from a party-plan event. Even though there is a business opportunity involved with direct selling companies, most partygoers know they are attending to buy a product and socialize with friends. They have not usually been offered a business. In network marketing, we invite people to learn about our products and make it clear that a business venture will be included in the offering. This is why building the list is slightly different. However, the concept of getting the wheels turning remains the same. One person writes while the other person is looking up.

Making a list might sound something like this: "So let's get started. Let's make your list together. If you won a trip for ten people today, which ones would you want to travel with you?" Or "Who are the five smartest businesspeople you know?" Many leading questions should be considered when assembling a prospect list for the first time. Here are just a few more ideas.

"Who do you know who knows everyone in your town? Who should run for mayor?"

"Who sold you your last home?"

"Who does your taxes?"

"Who watches your dog?"

"Who has the party house on your street? Who always hosts the Super Bowl party?"

"Who are the five most entrepreneurial people you know?"

"Who do you know who has made money, lost it, made it, and lost it again?"

"Who is the hardest-working person you know?"

"Who do you know who is sick and tired of their boss?"

"Who do you know who has always dreamed of having their own business?"

"Who do you know who has never met a stranger?"

"Who do you know who wants to stay home with their kids?"

"Who do you know who would like to help his wife retire from her job?"

You get the idea. You are *leading* your friend or partner to visualize potential business builders and customers. If you do not have anyone with whom to work, then make the list yourself. Be fearless and thorough. The longer and more inclusive your list, the more excited you will feel about picking up that phone.

By the way, I believe the list should be *mobile*. It must travel with you. Your list is a work in progress. You are always adding people, making notes about your initial contacts and your "follow-ups" as well as crossing people off the list. If you do not have access to it, you will not make a few calls while you are waiting to pick up your child from school, when you are fifteen minutes early to an appointment, or when you are on your way home from work. Becoming familiar with your list, updating it constantly, and adding names every day is a required business practice in expanding a networking business.

Now you have your "starter" list, which is long and chock-full of potential. Now it is time to pick up the phone, but what in the world will you *say?* This is where the rubber meets the road!

THE INVITATION

I am thinking back to 1990 when my mother bought a fund-raising franchise here in Orange County. I was her one and only sales representative. My mom taught me that I had to have a goal each time I picked up the phone, walked into a school to make a cold call, or sat down for a meeting. She trained me to pause slightly before every contact to determine what I wanted, set my intention, and imagine my desired result. Although I now do this unconsciously, it took me months and even years of training myself before it became a natural part of my process.

WHAT IS YOUR DESIRED OUTCOME?

Before you reach out to invite a friend to take a look at your business idea, take out a piece of paper and write down these words: "What is the desired outcome?" Take just a moment to determine what it is for you. Do you want your friend to come to your home on Tuesday night at seven to hear a presentation? Do you want to find a time to drop by her home after her kids have gone to school? Do you want to meet her near her office for lunch one day this week? Do you want her to watch a company video and call you back? What is it that you want? If you don't know what you want, why should you waste your time or hers? This is one of those things I do without thought. Make this a habit, and remember to teach it to others.

Remember one other thing before you pick up the phone. Although you are ready for this phone call and conversation, she may not be. She may or may not be having a fantastic day at the office. She may be in traffic or just running into the gym. She may have hung up the phone thirty seconds earlier after an altercation with her unruly teenager. This is nothing to worry about. There is nothing to fear. This could be the case even if you were just calling to invite her to a movie. This is where those "agreements" come in. Do not make assumptions, and do not take anything personally.

Always remember that your prospect will answer the phone in WIIFM mode: "What's in it for me?" We are all human. When we pick up the phone, we are asking, "Why are you calling? What do you need? Where is this going and why should I care?" People are not self-centered; this is simply the way we are wired. What I am going to cover now is vitally important in regard to this reality. My goal is to teach you to navigate the call without stress, anxiety, or fear.

AUTHENTICITY

There are a few simple ways to "disarm" your busy prospect. First, ask permission to proceed. Say something like "Hi, Ron. Carrie Dickie here. Do you have five minutes to talk? I have got something to share with you, but I want to make sure this is a good time." You need tons of confidence, conviction, and enthusiasm in your voice, yet you should be contained. You do not know what is going on in his world, and this call is all about him, not you. Do not overwhelm him with unbridled passion. Keep in mind that he is not as excited as you are yet.

After your friend or colleague has given you permission to proceed, "warm" him up. This is a necessary transition to bridge him from the world in which he was just present, to the world to which you are going to invite him. An easy way to do this is with a compliment. "You know, John, I have always admired your tenacity and passion for business."

Here are some other ideas for genuine compliments. By the way, that "genuine" part is critically important. People will know if you are only 99 percent sincere. Authenticity is 100 percent required. No patronizing. If the compliment does not ring true, you are finished. If you cannot come up with a genuine compliment, you probably are not ready to invite him into your business. You will be spending tons of time with this person if he decides to join you. It is important that you really admire him and desire to spend time in his presence. If you bring wonderful people to your business, your days will be awesome. You really want to have thinking, feeling, and heart-centered partners in your business. Let me offer a few more suggestions for openers.

- Theresa, I have always admired your wisdom and ethics in business and in life. You are someone with whom I can see myself working. When it comes to making money, do you keep your options open?

- Bob, you strike me as a visionary. You always seem to be ahead of the trends. I saw something the other day and thought of you immediately. When it comes to making money, do you still keep your business options open?

- Kurt, I have always admired your open mind when it comes to business. Would you consider meeting me after work tomorrow or Thursday to take a look at something I am really excited about?

Gaining permission to proceed and using the compliment approach are extremely beneficial in extending an invitation to people so they can learn more about what you have to offer. In doing this, remember that a person loves to hear his own name. Use a person's name and make it real and not forced. Do not use it every time, just enough. You will learn how much is enough. Check out the above invitations again and notice how much different they would sound without using the prospect's name.

FORM: FAMILY. OCCUPATION. RECREATION. MONEY. ASK QUESTIONS, LISTEN, MAKE THE CONNECTION, AND CREATE CURIOSITY

If you are calling someone with whom you do not speak very often, the approach may be a little different. You will not get permission to move forward with a conversation, drop in a compliment, and do the "invite." If you have not seen someone in six months or a year, it would be awkward to get right to it.

After the request for permission to move forward has been granted, you will say something like "Jane, I have a very specific reason for calling you this morning. I can share it right away or we can catch up for a few minutes. Which would you prefer?"

Or you might say, "Lisa, I came upon something the other day and thought of you immediately. I know we have not spoken for a while, since both of us have families and busy lives, but I have not been able to get you off my mind. I would like to find a time to catch up on your life and fill you in on mine. Could we get together and reconnect so I can share what I'm doing now? I think it might be right up your alley."

If you are not sure exactly how to connect, you can use FORM, an acronym for Family, Occupation, Recreation, and Money. You may gain permission to proceed, give a compliment, tell your prospect you have a specific reason for calling, and warm them up by asking a question in any one of these four areas. Here is an example:

> I know you are busy at work, and I appreciate these few minutes you have given me. Larry, I have always admired your positive attitude and your zest for life. You have been an inspiration to me for years. I have a specific reason for calling. It is a business idea I would like to share with you. First, though, I must ask, how are Mary and the boys?

Be sure to listen to his answer. Do not start thinking about what you are going to say next. Respond to what he says and show interest. His answer may reveal a problem in his life that might need solving. You might have just what he needs. If you do not ask questions and listen to the answers, you will never learn how you might be of help to him. He may say, "Wow, Carrie, it really has been a while since we have talked. Mary and I are separated." He may reply, "Things have changed since the last time we talked. Mary is doing well, but I am unemployed."

Although these words indicate that the timing may be good to share your business idea, do not jump the gun. Do not pounce on him and tell him that you have just the thing to help him get through it all. Be empathetic and patient, and ask more questions. Many times people are dying to share. Listen, listen, and listen some more. Be curious about them. Meet people where they are in life.

Sometimes things may be revealed in an initial conversation that will stop you from extending the invitation at all, because it is clear that your timing is wrong. Your contact may say something like "Hi, Carrie. It's great to hear from you. To tell you the truth, however, I am having a very rough day. My dad died yesterday, and I am making the arrangements and trying to get out of town tomorrow." A conversation like that will tell you much about your contact's current state of mind. Clearly it is not the right time to continue. You can console your friend and let them get back to their task at hand. Then follow up after an appropriate amount of time has passed.

If you contact a friend from college who has an entrepreneur-ial spirit and has experienced success in business, and you have been exchanging Christmas cards for years but only spoken a few times since you were in school together, the conversation will start out differently. After the initial pleasantries, you may say something like this:

> Tim, we have a lot of catching up to do and I am eager to do so, but I recognize that this may not be the best time. Would you like to catch up for just a few minutes, and then we can find another time to meet so that I can share the purpose for my call? I would really be interested to hear how your business is going, and I would love to know what those teenagers of yours are up to.

When you call people, ask things that invite conversation. Here's a list of ideas:

- How are your parents? Last time I checked, your dad was having some tests.
- How did that job interview go after we talked a few weeks ago? Did you get the job?
- How are you enjoying your new job? Is it everything you wanted it to be?
- Where are you and Charlene going for Christmas this year—or are you spending it at home?

- How are you enjoying your retirement? You sure worked hard, and I bet you are enjoying your freedom. Are you finding plenty to do?
- Last time we were together, you were expecting a big bonus check. Did it come through?

These questions show that you are interested in the lives of your friends, coworkers, and prospects. If you don't have the natural curiosity to ask these questions and many more like them, you will have to learn to do it. This is called connecting, and some people just do it naturally. If connecting is a challenge for you, you will need to start practicing everywhere you go. You need to make it your business to care. You need to practice learning about others, because it will help you grow your business and enrich your life.

In addition to making a connection with your prospect, the goal of the invitation is to create curiosity. You are hoping to say something interesting so they will want to know more. This is why it is so important to ask questions, listen to the answers, and make mental notes. You are looking for direction. Do not be afraid to pry. People rarely get to talk about themselves with someone who actually listens and cares.

TOP DOWN VERSUS BOTTOM UP

The difference between a top-down and bottom-up approach to building a network marketing business is just a matter of what information you share first with a prospect. Using the top-down approach, you share the Company story along with details about timing, trends, and the compensation plan. This is a business approach to building your team.

The bottom-up approach is different because you lead with your product. You may also share information about the business offering of your Company as well, but your primary focus will be the product offering. I believe it is most effective to start with what you are excited about. What ignites your passion and moves you? More importantly, what might your prospect be most open to hearing about?

In his book *How to Win Friends and Influence People* (1936), Dale Carnegie tells the reader to "bait the hook to suit the fish". I love this analogy. When you ask questions of your prospect, you are fishing. What's going on in their life? What is working and what is not? What do they want that they do not yet have? What makes them happy and what frustrates them? What are the details they are sharing that connect the two of you? How might your product solve a problem for them? How might your business work into their life? Keep asking questions and pay attention to their body language and what is not being said. This will give you direction when you get ready to share details of your opportunity. During this time, you are gathering information and showing compassion, empathy, and concern. If you are an effective "connector," you ask good questions, actually listen to the answers, and know exactly where to begin. If the cues do not come, then just ask them where they would like to start.

IT'S NOT ABOUT YOU—IT'S ABOUT THEM

Here is the most important point, and I cannot stress it enough. It is *not about you*. It is all about them! The focus is the person on the phone, sitting across from you during the coffee conversation, sitting next to you at the opportunity meeting, or sitting face-to-face via Skype. You are not trying to "get one". That is the Mars mentality that we sorely need to shift. On Venus, we are of service to one another. "How can I help you get what you want?" should be the question burning in your heart when you contact a prospect for the first time. As Zig Ziglar says, "When you help enough people get what *they want*, you will get what you want."

Wow. Isn't this what we want to be teaching our fellow Venusians?

BUILDING YOUR BUSINESS / COMPANY TRAINING / FINDING MENTORS / DOING WHAT FEELS RIGHT FOR YOU

The brilliance of network marketing is that you get to choose *everything* because you are in charge. The scary part of network marketing can be that you get to decide everything because you are in charge. If you have an involved sponsor or an active group in your area, you can plug into what is being offered around you. If nothing is going on in your area, you are a pioneer. You are *first*, and this can be a blessing if you choose it.

Most good companies have a training system you can plug

into. This is one of the awesome things about network marketing. The training is extremely inexpensive or free, and the people who are facilitating it have a vested interest in your success, especially if they share the Venusian mentality. People who help others (whether they receive financial compensation for doing so or not) understand that "a rising tide lifts all boats."

If I take the time to help you, whether or not you are in my group, someone somewhere will be helping one of my team members. This is a law of the universe. What goes around comes around; it is as simple as that. If you help someone become proficient at sharing the opportunity, they can offer another voice at your meetings, another perspective, another background, another example of success from which everyone can benefit. "Teaching people to teach people" is our job. Setting the example of generosity and cross-line support is a great way of moving this profession forward. This is the Venusian perspective in action!

Now, how is it most comfortable to build your business? Do you resonate with the idea of a home meeting? Do you like the idea of sharing the business via Skype each day from ten o'clock until noon when your kids are napping? Do you do most of your work on the phone because your circle of influence is in another state? Do you like to meet people one by one by one to make a stronger connection? I have done it all and it all works if you work it. Do the business the way it makes sense to you. Do it the way it feels right. After all, you are in charge. It is your business!

One of my mentors taught me the concept of plan, do, check, and adjust. Map it out. Execute. Assess the results and adjust the plan if necessary. In the beginning, you may do a lot of this. Remember—you will be bad before you are good, and good before you are great. You must be willing to step out of your comfort zone and try again and again. I love the saying "Life begins at the edge of your comfort zone." I could not agree more. Another one I love is "Do something every day that scares you." In the case of network marketing, that will make you money. And let's be honest, *making money may scare you.* Do you deserve to be free of financial burdens? Are you worthy of the life you are going to create for yourself? Be sure you have cleared the way for all the good that is about to come to you. If you do not, you will sabotage it. It is important to acknowledge this and own it if this is true for you. Help yourself by reaching out to a trusted friend, business partner, or mentor to talk about it. In fact, I am prompted here to include something from one of my mentors, Marianne Williamson in her 1992 book *A Return to Love: A Reflection on the Principles of a Course in Miracles.* This hit me right in the gut the very first time I read it years and years ago, and it continues to inspire me today.

> *Our deepest fear is not that we are inadequate. Our deepest fear is that we are powerful beyond measure. It's our light, not our darkness that most frightens us. We ask ourselves, who am I to be brilliant, gorgeous, talented and fabulous? Actually, who are you not to be? You are a child of God. Your playing small does not serve the world. There is nothing enlightened about shrinking so that other people will not feel insecure around you. We are all meant to shine as children do.*

We were born to make manifest the glory of God within us. It's not just in some of us; it's in everyone. And as we let our own light shine, we unconsciously give other people permission to do the same. As we are liberated from our own fear, our presence automatically liberates others.

You are here to be powerful, to shine, to lighten the load of others who walk beside you. When you know who you are and have claimed that you indeed are worthy of great things, you will be empowered to inspire others.

When you start out in network marketing, your goal is to create an engaging story. The easiest way to do this is to inspire a few people to try the products and to enroll your first business builder. Your goal is to do this quickly. As you bring in new people and recoup your initial investment, both of which are important elements for your story, other people become more and more encouraged.

You will discuss your top twenty prospects with your sponsor, upline partner, or friend and then reach out to them. *Together,* you will invite your friends, family members, and business colleagues to take a look at your new business idea.

MEETINGS

Whether or not you are comfortable, I recommend doing a home meeting right out of the gate, because this is a way of getting your feet wet *fast*. Since you will be sharing the business and products with at least a few people at this gathering, you are more likely to have some quick success, especially if you have a sponsor or side-line friend to help with the presentation.

Here are some ideas on how to get people to your home. You may be nervous about picking up the phone at first, so it is important that you make these calls right there with your sponsor. If geography makes that impossible, you can use the three-way call. The conversation to invite your potential guests to your home meeting is going to be short. You are in a hurry, *and* you do not want to answer a bunch of questions yet. You want to get a firm commitment and get off the phone. This is critical. Your only goal is to create curiosity and get them to your home. Remember to always give a compliment before you invite them. Tell them why you are choosing to reach out. Make them feel special, because they are. The following sample invitations should be used only after a legitimate compliment.

- John, remember you and I were talking the other day about how hard it has been to save money and to get ahead? We were discussing how the weekends go so fast and the weekdays go so slow? I have not been able to stop thinking about you, and I want to share something I have come upon that I believe is going to help me get some of my time back. I have a friend who is helping me change my situation, and he may be able to help you too. He is coming to my home this Tuesday night at seven for about an hour. Can you be there promptly at seven to listen to him for about forty-five minutes?

- Terry, I recently joined a Company that is bringing something very exciting to market, and I see huge profit potential. This may or may not be for you, and I want you to know I am not attached to your decision. My friend Jeanette, whom I admire and who knows a lot more about this than I do, will be at my house tomorrow night to give a thirty-minute business overview. Are you able to get to my home to hear about it from her?

- Linda, I have something you need to see. If you see the profit potential, it is something we can do together. If not, no problem, because I am not attached to your decision. I just want you to know what I'm so excited about!

- Dave, I have just come upon a Company in which I think you might be interested. I am working with some people whom I really admire, and I want you to meet each other. They are going to be at my home on Tuesday at six thirty. Can you be available for an hour that night to take a look?

I would like to call your attention to a few elements that are present in the invitations written above. In each invitation, something is included that tells your prospect why they should care. The question "What's in it for me?" is addressed and answered. Additionally, each invitation includes a call to action, a commitment to do something. You will need to add the other key elements to the recipe: conviction, enthusiasm, and urgency. If you have not yet developed your own personal version of these three elements, then listen to others and adopt a style that resonates with you.

When making your first calls, you will undoubtedly come upon people who cannot attend your home meeting. This is not a problem; just find another time that works for both of you to share your business. You may set up a time to meet with them personally or ask them to attend another business presentation a few days later. You should always be planning ahead, in case your prospects are not available on Tuesday night at seven. Right then and there may be best. As long as you are asking questions, sharing your Company's story, the product story, the timing story, and the concept of time freedom and residual income, you are doing your job. It really does not matter how you do it. You can use the in-home setting, the one-on-one presentation, the two-on-one coffee conversation, or the phone or computer, state-to state or country-to-country.

These are some of the main things we do on Venus to build our business. In contrast, here is something we do not do on Venus. We do not invite people to take a look at our business via e-mail or text. Think of e-mail and text as information, not communication. Do not send information to anyone or invite them to a meeting without first having a live conversation, in person or via Skype. You must at least share your business voice-to-voice on the phone. There is no substitute for real enthusiasm and a true connection. It is impossible to have the same level of communication via text or e-mail. This is a relationship business! You will never develop a meaningful network marketing relationship e-mail-to-e-mail or text-to-text.

ETIQUETTE: THE MEETING IS SET. NOW WHAT?

Assume that you have set a date for the in-home business briefing or the Skype meeting. The invitation has been given and people are coming. Let's take a few moments to talk about meeting etiquette and why it is so important.

Foremost, remember that we are in the business of duplication. Whatever you do will be noted and copied, whether you like it or not. Your potential distributors will not worry too much about what you say. What you do will have far more influence. You might as well start off doing things the right way, so that you're not backpedaling later on.

First of all, a meeting should start promptly, no more than five minutes after the scheduled time. If you set the precedent early, your team will follow suit later on. Starting on time shows that you are a professional and it honors people who arrive at the appointed time. If you follow this advice, you will already be more professional than 99.9 percent of the networkers out there. On Venus, punctuality matters. People's time is valuable. If you honor it, I promise you they will notice.

Second, the meeting should be simple and duplicable. People will make a note of everything you do and they will decide for themselves whether they want to do what you do. Water and a few finger snacks are appropriate. I like to have a little something out to eat for those people who are coming directly from work. It is best not to prepare fancy hors d'oeuvres with wine, or people may think, "I cannot afford to do this or I am not interested in doing this." Keep it simple and easy, and people will think, "Wow, maybe I can do this business." This is no big deal.

Third, the "official" part of a meeting should be no more than forty-five minutes start to finish. The most important part of the evening is the "meeting after the meeting," where everything happens. People enroll in the business, meet, mingle, and get connected. Confidence is built as stories and testimonials are shared. It's also a time for your guests to get ask questions and get answers. If your meeting starts late and goes on for two hours, the meeting after the meeting will not happen. If your meeting ends and people make a beeline for the door, then you have gone too long. The sign of a successful meeting is when you have to kick people out of your home.

Be sure the person in the front of the room maintains control. Save questions for the end of the presentation. The meeting should be a first glance at the business, not a deep study. If you get off track with questions, the meeting will run long. Remember that questions are answered at the end of the meeting.

Last, your meeting needs to be very much the same every time you do it, for a couple of reasons. First, it is important that people know what to expect every time they walk into your home. Knowing what to expect is key in building trust, belief, and confidence in the process. In addition, any successful networker knows how important it is to duplicate behavior. If people like what you do and trust that you will do it each time, they will feel comfortable bringing their prospects. They will also start to believe that they can do what you are doing. This is the magic of our profession. People can plug in and earn while they learn. If you constantly change it up and experiment with new tactics and procedures, people will lose faith. They will not have a clear vision of what is expected of them and how they will get there, so they will not commit. As you build your network marketing business, remember this: confusion is your enemy. Why? Because confused people do nothing. On Venus we build trust, we build relationships, and we plant our seeds in fertile ground, a place where others feel safe enough to put down their roots and grow.

9

YOUR TOOLBOX

NETWORK MARKETING IS 10 PERCENT mechanics and 90 percent mind-set. If you do not adopt a winning mind-set, it does not matter how proficient you become at inviting people to take a look at your business or how skilled you are at sharing your program and delivering a call to action. If you do not manage the thoughts that hover in the dark recesses of your mind, you will not get all that you potentially can from network marketing.

As I cover the nuts and bolts of building your business, I will frequently refer to the importance of developing a winning mind-set. It is impossible to overstate this point. I want to elaborate on what I think are the most important tools:

- your story
- the three-way call

- the home meeting
- the scripts
- following up and closing
- handling objections

YOUR STORY

You need to embrace your story. No matter how simple, insignificant, or embarrassing it may be to you, you need to be able to tell it with ease and confidence. I cannot tell you how many times a new network marketer has said, "Carrie, I really don't have a good story. My story is just not that exciting or unique." Not true. Everyone has a story that matters. Everyone has a meaningful story that will move other people to act. Since it is your story and your reality, it may not seem exciting to you. Nonetheless, we are all human, and our stories contain universal themes that weave us together, joining our hearts and minds. Your story is the initial part of the process that will connect you with others.

You will need to connect with a friend, sponsor, upline partner, or sideline associate to develop your story. What did you do before network marketing? How did you bump into this great profession? What moved you to take action? What was it like being you in the process? What is it like being you now? What does it feel like to walk a day in your shoes?

Your story needs to be written out. This is a nonnegotiable requirement. If I told you that your story could make or break your network marketing business, how much time would you spend crafting it? Well, this is exactly what I am telling you. Your story either grabs people or it does not. Every story has the potential to move people to act. You need to write down every detail and share it with someone. You need to read it to yourself, read it aloud, and read it to others. Then you need to whittle it down. You may be so close to your own story that you cannot even discern the amazing parts that will feed another until you go through this entire repetitive process.

Here is the goal: When you tell your story, it should prompt an internal dialogue with the listener. If they are bored, the story is not doing its job. They need to be silently saying things like "Wow, me too", or "I feel exactly the same way!" They might think, "Wow, I've been there", or "I can relate." Even if their path has been vastly different from yours, they will gain respect for you and who you have become, thinking, "This girl worked hard", or "This gal has courage and so do I." They need to be thinking, "Wow, if he can do this, maybe I can too," or "I have the same qualities he has. We might work well together." They need to feel a wide range of emotions while listening to you—perhaps angry, sad, joyful, and hopeful, all in the few minutes you share. Your story is the glue that will bind you together to navigate the network marketing journey with others in partnership.

Here is the story I share when I meet a prospect for the first time. I have told this story hundreds of times to thousands of people and have connected with many of them. It has taken me years to learn the importance of this remarkable tool in moving people toward the dreams of which they may have unconsciously let go.

As you read my story, please count the number of times that you feel connected to what I am saying, on any level. When I tell you that I hate wearing panty hose, and you are a guy, maybe you are remembering how much you hate wearing a tie!

Hey, Jim, thank you so much for sharing the details of your family, the job that you are currently doing, and the hopes that you have for your future. You have been really open, and I appreciate it.

Before I get to the details of our business opportunity, I would like to take just a few moments to tell you a bit about how I came to join this Company and, more important, how I came to see it as the vehicle by which I could realize some of the dreams I have had for myself since I was a young woman coming out of college.

I graduated from the University of Colorado in 1985 with a degree in advertising, and all I knew was what I did not want to do. I had no idea what I did want to do. I knew I did not want to work for other people and I did not want to wear panty hose.

I did not want to be a computer programmer or a flight attendant, and I certainly did not believe I was smart enough to be a doctor or an attorney. I put myself through school teaching fitness classes, doing personal training, and working as a bartender and waitress.

When I finished school, I moved from Colorado to California to seek my future. I immediately got a bartending job and taught classes at a fitness club. Within months, I pulled a quad muscle and did what other college graduates did back then: I searched the classifieds.

Over the next ten years, I sold books door to door. I was an outside sales rep for a temporary-help service like Remedy or Apple One. I helped my mom build a fund-raising business and worked in the schools. I worked really, really hard but never earned more than $40,000 in any year. I was a single woman trying to make ends meet. I packed half of a tuna sandwich and stopped at 7-Eleven for a carton of milk every single day after my lunchtime workout at Nautilus Plus. I remember when I was in Ross Dress for Less looking at a blouse that was thirty-two dollars. I wondered if there would ever be a time I could afford to buy something new to wear to work. I was broke.

I married Gordon at twenty-eight, and we had our two boys. He had a good job, so it did not matter that I didn't make much money. But I always wondered, "What in the world would I do if something happened to my husband?" I also had lots of friends who were young mothers who had left their careers to raise their kids. Because they had "careers," I always felt they had something to fall back on, whereas I had nothing.

Then one day a man came to my door and asked to meet Gordon. I invited him in and apologized because Gordon had apparently forgotten the meeting. This gentleman showed me his business and talked about residual income. I said, "Are you telling me that when someone sells vitamins in Iowa or Kentucky, I would get paid?"

He said, "That is exactly what I am telling you."

"Then sign me up." When my husband came home an hour later, I told him, "Honey, we have a new business!"

I quickly found out that my timing was off with that company. I was late to the opportunity. The fireworks had already gone off. However, I was fascinated with the business model and the introduction to network marketing. My business partners and I would sit around together and listen to audiotapes by Zig Ziglar, Denis Waitley, Tom Hopkins, Napoleon Hill, and Jim Rohn. Listening to them taught me the 80/20 rule: 80 percent of the people do 20 percent of the work, and 20 percent of the people do 80 percent of the work. And then they talked about the 1-percenters. I absolutely knew I was one of them. I longed to know what I could accomplish, and I was on fire to succeed. That was in 1992. I was with that company for about eighteen months when I threw in the towel. Even though I walked away from "the dream", I never forgot about network marketing.

I joined a direct selling company in 2005 and sold home décor items in women's homes. It was a party-plan company. I could not decorate my way out of a paper bag, but I loved the idea of building a team. I kept looking for the big, giant leader so I could "plug in," but she was really busy and a little detached. So I decided, "If it is going to be, it is up to me," and I began to run like the wind. I lived by the motto "Fake it till you make it," and it worked, although it took me years and years to achieve the title of "leader".

I finally aligned with my passion for health a few years later when I joined a network marketing company that promoted a health product that I loved. I had been a fish swimming in muck and mire for years. Now I was a fish swimming in water, and I became unstoppable. Before I knew it, I had thirty thousand people in my organization. Things were a lot of fun until it all fell apart when the economy shifted in 2008 and people could no longer afford my product. Additionally, the company made some bad business decisions, and everything started to unravel. Some elements that needed to be in that company were just not there.

At this point, I went within and lived by the motto "If I'm lying, I'm dying." I found I could no longer, with integrity, tell people that they could do what I had done. I simply didn't believe it anymore, and that was heartbreaking. I was "married" to that company and I did not want to "divorce" them and find another one, but I could not continue either. So I went away quietly, licked my wounds, and decided that I would never, ever open myself up to that kind of disappointment again.

I stepped out of the profession and focused on my home and family. I decided I was not meant to be a leader after all. Nobody was following me, and I felt as though I had let down everyone on my team. I felt responsible for the demise of my business. In fact, I felt responsible for the collapse of the entire company. I had no self-esteem, and at my core, I felt completely unworthy.

I was miserable. I felt like a failure and a fraud. Then I hired a life coach and started to clean up the dark places inside of me. I began to do inner work and learned about the thought patterns that were sabotaging me and dimming my light. I was thirsty for knowledge about how to heal my heart. I attended seminars and aligned with people who were on a similar personal growth journey, and I became fearless. When my coach told me to jump, I asked, "How high?" I was determined to feel whole and joyful.

One day a friend gave me a dream catcher, a tiny little vessel made out of clay. She told me to place my dream inside and put it on my altar. She said that my dream would come true, so I did what I was told. I wanted one thing more than anything else on the planet. I no longer cared about money or success, because they had not been the fix I had been looking for. I now had one goal in mind, which I wrote on a piece of paper and put inside that tiny clay pot where it still sits today. I wrote only two little words with big heartfelt meaning. That remains all I aspire to each and every day of my life. It reads, "Inner Peace".

Within eighteen months, I had peeled back quite a few layers of the proverbial onion. I was feeling excited, joyful, and free. I did not have a ton of money coming in, but I was sure that God was for me and that a bigger plan was yet to be revealed. I could not have been more right!

I wrote something in my journal on the morning

of June 13, 2010, and then printed and posted it in three places in my home. It said the following:

I am so happy and grateful that I have a career that feeds my spirit. It is wonderful to be connecting with people every day, helping them to reach their highest potential, and to achieve their goals. I am grateful to be able to work twenty-five hours per week and still be totally available for Gordon and the boys. I love what I do and feel so blessed to have found my niche.

People just come to me. They are drawn to me and to what I do. They are on the same amazing spiritual journey that I am on, and appreciate my expertise, my candor, my deep caring, and my ability. I am enthusiastic and look forward to jumping out of bed each day because this doesn't even feel like work! I am so blessed.

On June 18, 2010, just five days later, my dear friend of twenty-two years shared a company video that would change my life. On June 19, 2010, I joined yet another network marketing company, and I reached the top rank in the company in just twenty-two months. I tell people that "I built it," which is laughable. I partnered with powerful forces—God and the universe—and enlisted my friends. They enlisted their friends and the team was created—hour by hour, day by day, month by month, person by person, call by call, meeting by meeting, event by event, step by step, goal by goal, and heart by heart. I said yes in June 2010, and the rest was inspiration and dedication.

Well, that is my story, and now is the perfect opportunity to teach you what not to do. If I were to say all of this every single time, I would have people snoozing on tables with eyes glazing over, and I would probably never get to show the plan.

Here is the meat you can take off this bone. Use your judgment. Watch your prospect. Check out their body language. Make a note of their wants and desires, and decide how much of your story you will need to stimulate their desire. What can you share that will heighten their senses, open their minds and hearts, and strengthen your connection with them, so that they want to know more about what you have to offer? As my friend Wayne taught me a few years ago (and you will want to write this one down) if it's not necessary to say it then it's necessary not to say it.

There will be the occasional situation and person for whom your entire story will be perfect. Most of the time, however, you will need to adjust and abbreviate it. For example: I am sitting with a businessman with a 401(k), stock options, a big salary, no time, and three small children. He is sick and tired of being sick and tired because he travels overseas and lacks sleep, exercise, and healthful food. I will need to make my story concise. He will be centered in WIIFM mode (What's In It For Me?) and poised to grab on to any hope I can offer.

Hey, Jim, I want to thank you for letting me into your world for a few minutes. I appreciate all you've shared about your extensive travel, the fact that you do not see your family as much as you want to, and the hopes you have of gaining some of your time back. You are a good man who's determined to get his priorities in line.

Before I get to the details of our business opportunity, I would like to take just a few moments to tell you a bit about how I came to join this Company, and, more important, how I came to see it as the vehicle by which I could realize some of the dreams I had for myself when I was a young woman coming out of college.

I graduated from the University of Colorado in 1985 with a degree in advertising, and all I knew was what I didn't want to do. I had no idea what I did want to do. I did not want a boss, and I did not want someone else to control my time. I wanted choices. [Jim feels he has no choices. He's is in pain and has no time.]

I did not have the "straight line" career path that you have experienced. In fact, I have done a little of everything. I put myself through school bartending, waiting tables, and teaching fitness classes. I dabbled in the "real world" for about a year with an outside sales job and helped build a fund-raising company for a number of years. During that time, I married my husband, had two boys, and stumbled onto network marketing. I made a ton of mistakes and found out my timing was off. I was a little bit late to the barbecue, but I was fascinated by the thought of residual income and time freedom. [This may be getting painful for Jim as I connect to the angst and frustration of his situation.] Even though I have always worked hard, I never earned more than $40,000 in any year!

I found the profession again in 2005, which allowed my husband to retire in 2008. I make more money today in two weeks than I used to earn in a year, but the best part is that I am free. If I need to "unplug" to take care of a family member or one of my kids, I can do so. If I take a month-long vacation to Tahiti, I can leave my phone and computer in the hotel. As it stands now, I can conduct my business from any location in the world as much or as little as I desire. I have true financial freedom and the time to enjoy it. [I add some last thoughts to highlight the problem and then offer a potential solution.]

Wow, what a difference in the presentation of the two stories, eh? It's the same story, but the feel is totally different. I hope you grasp the importance of creating a version of your story that will move the prospect to act! This will take practice, practice, and more practice, but you will get it.

After every one-on-one meeting, two-on-one coffee conversation, or group meeting, you need to evaluate your skill level. Remember to plan, do, check, and adjust. You planned it and did it, so now assess it and make the changes necessary to increase your effectiveness. After a presentation during which you sat in the audience and heard someone else present, be sure to evaluate how well they did in connecting with the group. Did they say things that elicited the responses you wanted to see from your prospect? Did they talk about themselves with little consideration for how the prospects might identify with them? Did they sound humble and grateful (Venus) or condescending and arrogant (Mars)?

I cannot tell you how many times I got to the end of a one-on-one only to find my prospect glassy-eyed and ready to bolt. I quickly realized that I had not taken the time to connect, and to assess his needs and areas of concern. I motored forward with my presentation, complete with jokes and witty banter. Then I suddenly realized I had gotten carried away—literally "Carrie'd" away! I made it all about myself and what I thought he wanted. I talked at him and not with him.

Here's the bottom line. Your story matters. It is an extremely important part of your journey. You are creating your story each and every day in network marketing. Be sure it is something of which you can be proud. Be sure you stay inspired and inspiring. Your story needs to be authentic and real. Remember—people are not joining your Company. They are not joining the business for your products. People are joining you.

If you are not someone whom people want to follow and be around, this business will be quite difficult for you. You have no idea who is going to stick with this business opportunity and make it big. We are all human. We may look similar from the outside, but we have no idea what lives inside another person. We have no idea who will turn themselves inside out to become charming, witty, helpful, authentic, and selfless to rise to the top and lead their tribe. That is one of the biggest blessings I have experienced in this profession. I have watched shy people become bold, scared people become fearless, defensive people become receptive, and broken people become wealthy and whole. This is one of the benefits. I hope and pray you get to witness this for yourself one day. Maybe you already are! If so, I congratulate you and I am grateful for you too. On Venus, we celebrate everyone's success. The more people who get to the top of our profession, the better we become. Wouldn't it be a loss to get to the top of your Company without becoming?

THE THREE-WAY PHONE CALL
THE POWER OF THIRD-PARTY VALIDATION

We have covered the importance of crafting and presenting your story in a manner that inspires another person to act. Now let's examine another powerful tool in the network marketing toolbox.

The three-way call is one of the most effective means of connecting the dots for any prospect who is evaluating your Company for the first time. Before I dive into the mechanics of the three-way, let's first talk about when to use it and why it can be so effective, and let's clear up a few misconceptions about one of this profession's most underused power tools.

As I have said before, it can be difficult to get started in network marketing. If you are a professional in another business arena, it can be even harder, especially if your profession has the typical hierarchical structure in which position is often a function of tenure and level of education. Network marketing is a level playing field that offers prosperity to anyone with courage and a coachable orientation. If you are a successful real estate broker, insurance agent, or medical professional, you may seriously struggle with the idea of allowing your "truck driver" sponsor to "get at" your clientele. You may get stuck in your ego (like they do on Mars) and determine that you are much smarter than your "waitress" upline partner, and that you certainly cannot trust everything she is attempting to teach you. You may silently say something like, "She has no idea how I run my business. This three-way call thing is not going to fly with my people. I need to make it look more professional. Perhaps a PowerPoint presentation at my office with a guy in a suit would gloss over the fact that this is a network marketing gig."

This can be what new people say or at least think. After all, they have reputations to protect, right? People respect and admire them, and they do not want to appear unhappy or unsuccessful in their current business. After the starter kit has been purchased and the commitment has been made, the ego often jumps in to run the show.

Let me make my point another way. Imagine you are standing on one side of a giant black tunnel in the middle of nowhere and you are desperate. Why? Because everything you desire is on the other side of the tunnel. There is just one problem. You are absolutely terrified because you are afraid of the dark! You know you are thinking too much. Your self-talk goes something like this: Millions of others have walked through this tunnel before me. To get what I want, I have to walk through. There's no other way. Over and over you tell yourself, "Just do it!" But you are frozen still. Suddenly a guide appears out of nowhere and offers his hand. He says, "Let me help you. I've been to the other side and I can help you walk through. It is not that scary. I have done it. Let's walk together."

When you are a new distributor, making those first calls to "reach out and touch someone" can be as scary as walking through that dark tunnel. However, when a sponsor is right there offering the three-way call, it can provide that little push you need to pick up the phone, which moves you one step closer to your dreams.

The three-way call should be used immediately, before your mind gets into the mix and starts that discouraging inner dialogue: Don't follow them. You could fall. I wonder if they have really done this before. They might not know what they are doing. You could be stuck in the dark. You could die! If your new distributor cannot see the light at the end of the tunnel, they are not likely to enter the tunnel alone. However, if they know that you are there to support them and field the questions for which they don't yet have the answers, they are more likely to push through. They will be willing to respond to their prospect with "I don't know," as long as they can also say, "I can get the answer right now. Let's call someone who does know."

Whether you are brand new to the profession or have been in it for years, the three-way call is a critical piece of your success puzzle. This is why you should not delay in making those initial calls and invitations for the first in-home presentation and two-on-ones with your sponsor and prospects. These successful initial interactions will result in forward movement right out of the gate.

The confidence with which a sponsor, friend, or guide approaches your first three-way call will determine your comfort level. They will be likely to proceed with calm clarity. They have very little fear, since they have made lots of calls. Also they do not know your prospect personally. They probably do not have any history with your prospect and you are not likely to share common friends. So there will be no preconceived notions or attachment to what the prospect's level of interest will be. Thus, this call will be a no-brainer for them. This third-party validator is not biased in any way and typically has much less fear. They will be calm, confident, and able to share the message and answer questions with ease and grace. This is what makes the call so effective. They play the role of an outside consultant validating the things you may have already shared. It is not that you are not trusted by your prospect. Rather, it is about being validated by someone outside of the sphere in which you may know them. You will be able to relax, listen and take it all in. You will learn by observing and listening. The more you learn, the better you will do on future calls. Three-way calling will provide the ongoing training you need to build your business and give others the confidence they need to do the same.

Some people mistakenly believe the three-way calling method is used just until you get proficient at sharing the story. They use it for a week or two, but stop as soon as they have most of the answers. To some degree, I understand why you might consider dropping this tool. After all, you know nothing in the beginning, so you need your validator. You work the business together every day, and you gain the knowledge and experience to respond effectively to questions. Your awareness of what you don't yet know heightens your sensitivity to rejection or hesitation from the prospects. However, after a few weeks and a lot of calls, you have increased your knowledge and confidence appreciably, and you think you can now make these calls on your own. Here's the rub. If you contact a new prospect and do not model the three-way call, the prospect may be extremely intimidated by the amount of knowledge you have acquired. They may conclude, "I cannot do what she just did. I cannot possibly pick up the phone and talk to my brother, mother, friend, or coworker and answer all the questions that I just asked." This approach makes it look like you got into the business and knew it all right out of the gate. This is a Martian approach: "I can build this all by myself. I do not need anyone!" Instead, model the behavior of asking for help and receiving it. This is the way of the Venusian, and it is far more duplicable.

Please read carefully and highlight the next sentence. The three-way call is a tool that you will use for the rest of your career. You will never be out of the business of duplication. This tool will always be required. However, there will come a time when the three-way call is less about sharing the details of your program and answering questions, and more about making connections and building relationships. Additionally, people never want to work in a vacuum, without the support and power of the team. The beauty of our profession is that we are in business for ourselves, but not by ourselves. This camaraderie opens people's hearts and seals them into the business. The constant support and involvement from other like-minded people, coupled with their own dreams and desires, propel the new person to tackle their fears head-on. This is the heart-centered approach we use on Venus.

THE PROSPECT—THE BRIDGE— THE THIRD-PARTY VALIDATOR

Again, the three-way is used as a bridge between you, as a brand new distributor, and your prospect. It will help you learn the details of your opportunity. In this process of listening to the validator on these calls, you learn about your Company's products, story, and marketing plan. This may take weeks or even months, depending upon how fast you are able to move forward. You will continue to use the three-way call in every stage of assembling your network. It builds belief, establishes relationships, and reveals strengths and weaknesses so that partnerships can be created for the greatest advantage to the team.

The power of another viewpoint cannot be overemphasized. There is just something magic about hearing the same message from another voice, another perspective, and through the power of another person's story.

This personal anecdote will illustrate the inherent power of having an outside validator. I suspect that you have had this experience yourself in some shape or form. As a young woman, I was a fitness trainer, aerobics instructor, and waitress/bartender. I jumped like I had springs on my feet. I taught high-impact aerobics classes and had my share of dangerous falls with trays of food and drink in my hands. I played years of tennis as a young mother, trying to channel the stress of raising two boys under the age of two. At the age of forty, my body was pretty taxed by the time I found Bikram yoga. And, coupled with the hot room, Bikram yoga helped me put Humpty Dumpty back together again! I am so grateful to have found it when I did.

My husband, Gordon, was an avid soccer player at the time, and his knees were giving him trouble. I talked almost daily about the therapeutic benefits of Bikram yoga and how it was helping me. I told Gordon again and again about the surfers and soccer players who were in my classes; I suggested he come to class with me to check it out. For a long time, I don't think he ever gave it a second thought. Then one day he popped into the house after work and said, "I'm running up to change. I'm going to yoga with Tony."

I said, "You're going to yoga with Tony? My yoga?"

He said, "Yep. Tons of people are using it to help them in their sport. Even professional soccer players are using it to minimize their injuries." I was floored. I had been sharing this message with him for years. Yet it took just one "on the fly" invitation from his friend Tony, Gordon's outside validator, and he was all about it. All of a sudden, Tony was the expert! Gordon continued to attend yoga classes, mostly without me, long after Tony quit going.

This story dispels one of the common misconceptions about the three-way call, which is that the third party must be an expert who is much more experienced than you. It's not so. The three-way call is used to make your business accessible to everyone. Think about it. What did Tony say to Gordon that day that I had not said? What did he share that I had not been sharing for years? I had read the book and knew every posture. I was even thinking about going to Los Angeles to do the nine-week teacher training for $5,000. It was not my expertise that got Gordon to yoga. It was the alchemy of the same story from a different voice, plain and simple.

We do three things in network marketing. We expose people to our products and business offering, we promote from event to event, and we build community. One of the most effective ways to build community—day after day, week after week, and year after year—is to use the three-way call. Do not try to build your business without it.

THE MECHANICS OF THE THREE-WAY CALL

One of the reasons the three-way call is underused in network marketing is because many people are not confident about how the call should be done for maximum effectiveness. For the benefit of anyone who struggles with this, I am going to break down its elements.

One of the biggest sources of confusion is how to set up the call. If you do a good job setting it up, the call can be extraordinarily effective. But if you botch the setup, the call may fall flat. Let's talk about the two basic ways to lead into an effective three-way call.

In the first example, you will alert your prospect to the possibility of a third-party call during the invitation, by saying something like this:

> John, I have something you have got to see. I have always respected your head for business. Do you have a few minutes to take a look? I have someone here whom I admire and trust. If you like what you see online, I would like to introduce the two of you. If not, no worries—I am not attached to whatever you decide. Is there a chance you are free for the next thirty minutes or so?

In this invitation, you are complimenting your prospect and alluding to the presence of another bright businessperson waiting in the wings to expand on the offering. What a brilliant way to grab the prospect's attention and create urgency and curiosity. This is the perfect way to share your business idea when you are brand new and short on knowledge and confidence. You have the relationship with your prospect, and you are empowering your upline business partner with words such as admire and trust. If your prospect shows interest, you have already set the stage for further discussion without the potentially awkward introduction of a third party.

The other way to set up a three-way call is after you have made the initial invitation and shared some preliminary information. This could still be during your first conversation, though it could also be on the second or even third. You might be more comfortable with this approach after you have learned a few details about your program and how to share it with others, in addition to learning a bit more about the prospect's areas of interest. This sifting and sorting approach delays bringing another person into the mix until you have a prospect who has expressed interest. You could use one method for one situation and the other method in another. What matters is not how you bring in the third party, but that you do it and that you accomplish it with ease and grace. Remember to be patient with yourself and others. I have already made you aware of the steep learning curve!

When you are talking one-on-one with your prospect by phone, Skype, or in person, you need to be as natural as possible. Relaxed authenticity will serve you and override your lack of experience. Being real will compensate for your mistakes. If you are nervous and agitated, or you timidly ask permission to bring another person into the conversation, your prospect's natural warning radar will go off. Conversely, if you are confident, excited, and self-assured, people will follow you anywhere. When they ask you a question and you candidly reply, "Hmm that is an excellent question. Let me get my friend Pam to answer that one for us. I want to know too," your prospect will stay more engaged and open. People want to be skillfully led. They do not want to be pushed and pulled. The difference is subtle but important. Only time and practice will increase your skill level. I urge you to get good at executing the setup of the three-way call. It will pay off in many ways.

At this point you have shared a bit about your business, or you have shared a lot of information, and your prospect is showing interest in learning more. Now it's time to bring in the third party, who will deliver the same message with a different voice, a different style, and a different story. The addition of another person adds interest, variety, and validation to the opportunity you have brought to your prospect's attention. If your prospect is even moderately interested in what you have, they will likely be open to hearing another perspective.

Be sure that you are assembling a list of people to validate for you. The people on this list will provide support by telling the story of how they found your Company, what they love about it, and how it has helped them solve a problem they had before becoming involved. You should have a number of people on your three-way calling list, so that you will be able to reach the right someone most of the time. It is important to put a little bit of thought into each of these calls. When you orchestrate a three-way call, you need to decide which colleague your new prospect might enjoy talking with the most. You need to choose a "validator" who will effectively deliver the message you want your prospect to get. Ideally you'll select someone with whom your prospect will identify, so that they'll have a point of shared experience. You may also have a validator on your list that is good at finding a connection, no matter what. This is typically your sponsor or upline leader. They will work hard to find a connection point from which to initiate and facilitate a meaningful business conversation.

You should always text or call your list of validators ahead of time, to let them know that you are preparing to make calls, because you need to know in advance who is available. Do yourself a favor and avoid the potential embarrassment that arises when you have created a good setup for the three-way but cannot connect with the validator. Remember this is your business. People are joining you, and they want to be confident in your modeling and leadership.

Your list of validators is important, since you may not have immediate access to your sponsor or upline leader. You might need to attend a local meeting and make some new friends to add to your three-way calling list. Similarly you might reach out at the next big event and connect with some new people to expand your list of contacts. Knowing distributors from all over the country is extremely smart in our business. Being of service to other networkers that you meet at events will ensure that you always have someone to call on when you need help building your business from state to state. Model what you want other people to do, because what goes around comes around.

Despite your preparation, sometimes you will be unable to facilitate that three-way call right then and there, and that's okay! Just set up a later time. No worries. Take a breath and know that if your prospect is interested, you cannot say the wrong thing, especially if your intention is authentic and sincere. Be yourself, share from your heart, and set up the call for another time. We are in the business of duplication. Don't duplicate stress and anxiety or strive for perfectionism. Be gentle with yourself and others. Let things develop and allow them to fall into place. This is how we do it on Venus!

THE INTRODUCTIONS DURING THE THREE-WAY CALL

The proper introduction of all parties involved in a three-way is absolutely key. Grab your pen and write this one down, please. Always introduce the prospect first! Why? They are the most important person in the mix. The call is all about them, and you must not forget it. They will love hearing their name and all of their amazing attributes you are about to share. Always give wonderful and valid compliments and details about your prospect, to make them feel special. You don't need to patronize your prospect. Instead, share details about how you met, married, worked out, partied, played, vacationed, or lived together. Explain to your third-party validator why this prospect must join you in your business. Be passionate, funny, and real. If you can't get excited about introducing your prospect, you should not be inviting them at all.

Then do the same for your third-party validator, but be careful. You need to go softer here. Do not inflate and exaggerate. Do not set up your third-party validator to fail by building them up too much before they even open their mouth. You do not want your prospect rolling their eyes, drumming their fingers, or saying, "Enough. Let's get this ball rolling." Let me give you an example of an effective three-way call setup.

> Hey, Jennifer, I have Linda on the line. Linda is one of my dearest friends in the world. We go way back. She and I have known each other for many years. In fact, Linda and her husband got married three months before Gordon and I did, nearly twenty-five years ago. We have been through a lot together, and we are very close. Linda is smart, accomplished, and open to looking at our business. She was very successful in the field of human resources before we both had kids, and she is excellent with people. Her kids are both in school now, and she's giving some thought to going back to work in some capacity.
>
> Linda, this is my new friend Jennifer. She is awesome, energetic, and fun to be around. I met Jennifer at the gym a few months ago, and we have been working together on this new project ever since. She has two kids like we do, and she's building a successful business from home. Jennifer, I want you to meet my longtime friend Linda. And Linda, I want you to meet this remarkable businesswoman and my new friend, Jennifer.

The purpose of the introduction is to create connection and lay the foundation for a conversation. Your introduction should be energetic, concise, and clear. Ego and power are not how we invite people into our business. I am talking about a well-thought-out introduction, full of interesting bits of information and talking points with which to connect. If you look back at this sample introduction, you'll see that there are several things with which the validator can engage. Maybe it's the twenty-five-year marriage, or perhaps the career in human resources. Maybe it is the gym connection or the idea of building a business from home. If you do a good job of paving the way, a meaningful conversation will flow. Both parties will feel comfortable, open, and willing to move forward.

DURATION OF THE THREE-WAY CALL

Another challenge with the three-way is its length. Often people will spend an hour or more on the phone, but you should try to keep it succinct. This call should last no more than twenty minutes, unless your prospect demonstrates extreme interest. Always think of duplication. People who have "real jobs" cannot validate for an hour at a time. People who have small kids at home will rarely find an hour to stay engaged on the phone. At least one of the people on the three-way call will likely need to get off the phone, but may hesitate to tell you so. Be aware, tune in, and make sure that everyone is good to go before the call becomes too lengthy for anyone. You may scare a busy prospect away before they ever take a good look at your business, just because you spent too much time on this call. It's often a good idea—at the end of the introductions, for example—to set a time expectation. Something similar to: "Linda and Jennifer, I know your time is valuable. I think we should be able to cover this in about fifteen minutes or so. Does this work for both of you?" That is a professional and considerate way to move forward.

GOALS FOR THE THREE-WAY CALL

The last point for consideration is the importance of having a goal for the three-way call. You must always be at least one or two steps ahead of your prospect. The first exposure is the initial invitation to take a look at your offering. The second exposure may be a Company video. The third exposure may be the three-way call. As you approach the end of the three-way, you must know where you want your prospect to go next. Is it a home meeting in the local area, so that your prospect can get a feel for the people with whom you are involved? Is it a training event coming up in a few days? Do you want your prospect to join you and your sponsor for a cup of coffee tomorrow morning to answer more questions? Do you have some homework for the prospect to do before you meet again? Knowing where you want them to go, and skillfully leading them toward the next steps, will instill confidence and belief in your prospect. They will want to follow you if it feels right. You may need to have a brief conversation with your validator before the call, so that you both know where you are headed. However, be sensitive to everyone's time. Be efficient, confident, and authentic. These three ingredients will contribute to an excellent recipe for success!

A FEW DO'S AND DON'TS ABOUT PROSPECTS

- Please don't invite unfriendly people to join you, no matter how apparently successful they seem.
- Do not push people into joining your business. It is a delight to work with those who are yearning to grow, learn, and expand their horizons.
- If someone is greedy and self-absorbed, and they enjoy being that way, then please do not invite them to join network marketing.
- It is best to recruit up. Invite people who are smarter and more successful, connected, evolved, and humble than you are. They will challenge you, stretch you, strengthen you, and bless you with their skill, talent, and charm.

To recap, the goal for every three-way call is to create connection, which will build belief and trust. Connection can bolster the prospect's confidence in your Company's system of training and duplication. The prospect may think, "Wow, if she can pick up the phone and get my questions answered, then I might be able to call a friend *and do the same*." The prospect may go even further, if you have facilitated a good call, and think, *"I am not going to be in this alone. I am going to have help, because these people have a vested interest in my success. If they help me get what I want, they will get what they want. This is a great business in which to be a partner."*

You may have a prospect who will not want to meet anyone until they have turned over every stone. No worries. Let them be your guide. Suggest a three-way call, but if they reject that idea, move on to another method of exposure. The three-way call is just another tool in your toolbox. Pull it out when the time is right. The more practice you have using it, the more skilled you will become.

THE HOME MEETING
Getting Grounded

I am excited to talk about the party, which was another big "why" for my joining network marketing. I loved getting out of the house, and I was excited to go where the action was, so I went to opportunity meetings to get invigorated. I just love people. I love to learn about them and ask them questions. I love to look for commonality and what makes them different from me. I love to know what makes people tick.

My life coach once asked a group of us to identify our spiritual "food" and to share our insights. People came up with marvelous answers, reminding me what a rich playground we inhabit here on planet Earth. They shared things such as the sun and moon, oceans and mountains, music, dancing, bird-watching, gardening, and spending time in nature. I, too, am fed by some of those things, but the answer that sprang from my lips was "people". My spiritual food has always been people. I'm fascinated, intrigued, mesmerized, and perplexed by them. I am challenged and lifted and taught by them. I am surprised, disappointed, inspired, blessed, energized, exhilarated, empowered, and enlightened by people.

There was a time when I wanted to be around people all the time. It did not matter where we were going or what we were doing; I just wanted to be included. Today, it is the individual person who fascinates me. One-on-one conversation or small-group interaction is lovely. I yearn to know what you yearn for. I have a longing to learn from you. I wake up each day knowing I will be connected with people who will inspire me, stretch me, and bring out the best in me. I am excited to know where I am going, what I am going to do, what I am going to say, and to whom I will say it. I often wonder, *"What am I going to learn today?"*

I am trying to make an important point. In network marketing, as in life, you must take great care in managing yourself and your energy. People are drawn to you or repelled by you. They either want to be around you or they wander away. They will stick around or not, which may or may not be a conscious decision on their part. An energy field surrounds you, extending about ten feet in every direction. Since birds of a feather flock together, why not take the time to ground yourself every day and work on being the type of person you want to attract to your life and business? On Venus, we *care* about such things. We do not change ourselves for other people; we just work hard to stay in alignment with who we really are at the core, so that people can see us and choose us. We know that people will not want to join us if we show up in a way that is not congruent with whom we were born to be. Venusians long to be seen and appreciated for who they truly are.

Be aware that humans are judgmental by nature and that first impressions are important. Ask yourself, *"How am I presenting myself to the world today?"* If your business is about wellness, you should exude health and vitality. If your business is about financial integrity, it's important that you are financially "true".

I have seen a lot in the last couple of decades. I have seen overweight men with bad breath and body odor selling health and wellness. I have seen young people in shredded jeans and trendy shirts attempting to prospect successful businessmen. I have seen beautiful women showing too much leg and too much cleavage giving meetings in front of rooms and attempting to make a good impression on the wives of the men with whom they are working. I have been backed up against the wall with men and women so close that I was afraid a stray spit spot would end up on my face or, even worse, in my mouth. We sometimes forget about personal space in the rooms where we gather.

I am trying to tell you to mind your energy. Pay attention to the signals you are putting out. Are they in alignment with the business you are sharing with your prospects? Are you the person you are presenting to the world? Are you clean and neat, with good personal hygiene, presenting yourself in a way that you want to be seen by others? Are you able to look at yourself objectively? I encourage you to ask a few people whom you trust, "How can I better share the "me" I want people to experience? Can you make any suggestions?"

We are going to talk about the home meeting, a vital tool in building your business. It's accessible to almost everyone, yet underused. The home meeting is critical in building a successful network marketing business, and yet the mechanics are not always taught. Let me inspire you to use this powerful tool.

People will join you only if they feel *safe*, and they will feel safe only if you are *real*. If you are who you say you are, people will be excited to come to your home, build a business together, and invest time in developing a relationship with you. But if people cannot trust and respect you, they will not do any of these things.

Be authentic and real. Manage your energy. Put your best foot forward. You are a networker now. How you show up every day *matters*. Be the person you would want to follow. Ask yourself, *"How do I want to be perceived today? What is my energy telling people about me today?"*

GROUP SPONSORING

In preparation for home meetings, I would like to introduce you to what I believe is the most powerful force in network marketing. The most powerful tool you have at your fingertips is the power of the group. When you enter your Company, if the group is already assembled, that's fantastic. If not, then fantastic again! If meetings are already being held in your area, you have an instant support system. At those meetings will be people you can identify with and work beside. If there are not yet meetings in your area, then congratulations, because you are first, and you get to set the tone for the events that take place there. The power of the group cannot be overemphasized!

Here in Southern California, our group meetings often take the form of "beach bonfires". We swim, surf, and play music. We play football, soccer, and Frisbee™ until the sun goes down. At sunset, our families cook hot dogs on sticks and roast marshmallows. When the sun is gone, it can get a little chilly, so we sit around the fire to keep warm. These group meetings are a little bit of heaven, and we tend to hang around that fire until the bitter end when the beach closes at ten o'clock.

On those evenings at the beach, every log contributes to the power and intensity of the fire. Each log's flame is stronger when joined with the flame of another. The beauty of the bonfire is the collection of logs, flames, coals, and embers that contribute to its intense power. People get tired, more reflective, more grateful, and more serene as they gaze into the fire and see the faces of those gathered on the other side. Kids snuggle into their parents' laps and stay close to the group for warmth and connection.

At about nine forty-five, the beach patrol drives by and everyone contributes to breaking it all down. Towels are shaken out, swimsuits are put away, and coolers, beach chairs, and Boogie BoardsTM are loaded into cars. The very last thing to deal with is that beautiful fire, which has been burning for hours and is hot, hot, hot. Left alone, a fire is dangerous, so our job is to completely extinguish it. How do we do that quickly and effectively? We separate the logs, creating space between them, and they quickly lose their heat. With just a few foot stomps and a little bit of sand cover, the fire is out. This story illustrates my point about the potential of the group. The fire is powerful and generates a ton of heat, as long as each log remains in the pit. Only when the logs are separated does the fire diminish until it is finally extinguished.

Network marketing is exactly like that fire. People are stronger together, empowered by the energy and passion of one another. We "feed" each other with our stories of strength, hope, success, struggle, pain, and the ability to overcome. Only when we stray too far from the fire pit is our commitment tested, our belief questioned, and our success in jeopardy. Our fire burns hot and bright for everyone to see. Together we are unstoppable.

I will often tell a new person to catch themselves on fire with enthusiasm, and people will come from miles around to watch them glow. This could not be more true. People yearn for purpose and passion in their lives. They are hungry for light and enthusiasm in their world. We are each drawn to the fun, the laughter, and the hope. Venus is full of joy, peace, and possibility. A network marketing business is like that bonfire. Someone had to envision it, believe in it, build it, start it, stoke it, fuel it, and continue to feed it. Someday that fire will practically burn of its own volition. Keep your fire burning and help your teammates when they do not yet know how to build a fire of their own. They will learn because you will teach them. Soon they will have their own parties with their own families in attendance, sitting around fires and sharing stories of hope and freedom with one another. I dream this for you. I believe this for you. I know this is possible for each and every one of you.

Now let me elaborate on the concepts of group sponsoring, the home meeting, and the power of the team!

THE HOME MEETING

The home meeting is one of the most powerful tools in your network marketing toolbox. Let's talk about the psychology of the home meeting. First, your home is a reflection of who you are. Inviting people to join you in your home is a somewhat intimate gesture. Unlike a one-on-one at the coffee shop or a larger hotel meeting, the home meeting is a personal invitation into your world. I encourage you to treat it as such. Take the home meeting seriously, and people will respect it. How do you set the tone for a fun, informative, and effective meeting in the space you call your home?

SCHEDULING—TIMING

First, it is important to schedule this meeting in your home right out of the gate. Put it on the calendar the day you enroll as a distributor with your Company. The universe likes swift, immediate, and decisive action on your part. It will respond in kind. If you are serious, choose a date that is no more than a week to ten days out. The sooner you have your first meeting, the sooner you will see the first leaves growing on the tree called your business. Here is a good example of the need for *urgency* in scheduling your first home meeting:

It's the morning of Monday, June 1, and I have scheduled my first meeting for the evening of Friday, June 12. I call you:

> Good morning, my friend! It's Carrie Dickie here. Have I caught you at an okay time? Listen, I have come upon something you have to see. I know you are going to be fascinated. I thought of you because you have such a discerning eye for business. I am having someone over to my home on June 12 for an hour or so to share the details. Are you able to come over then to hear more?

First of all, most people will not commit to events happening ten days out. They will likely say, "Hmm sounds interesting. Tell me more about it." Why in the world would anyone be expected to wait ten whole days to learn more details? Further, they are likely to answer with "Let me check my calendar, and I will get back to you." It is nearly impossible to get a commitment when the date is so far in the future. Also, there is that thing called urgency, which is massively lacking in scheduling a meeting nearly half a month away. Let's look at another scenario.

Again it's the morning of Monday, June 1, but this time I have chosen Thursday, June 4, for the first gathering in my home. It's just three days away! I call you on the phone:

Oh my goodness, I am so glad you picked up. I was praying that it would not go to voice mail [urgency]. My friend, I have always admired your keen eye for business, and I have got something you must see. I think you are going to be impressed. I am having a few people into my home [intimacy] on Thursday night at seven o'clock, just three days from now. Can you come over for just an hour to hear more about this opportunity?

Alternatively you can lead with your product. Here's an example:

Jane, it is Carrie. Have I caught you at a good time? Awesome. Listen, I have come upon something I am really excited about, and I have just got to share it with you. You know how we are always talking about not having energy in the afternoons when the kids come home from school? Well, I have found my answer. Are you by chance able to come over here this Thursday [just three days from now] at seven o'clock for about an hour? Honestly, this could change our lives. You are going to be so excited when you hear about this!

Just feel the difference in the two invitations. The intensity and enthusiasm can be the same, but the message will *never* come off the same when the meeting is not happening for ten more days. An invitation conveys no urgency at all when the date is too far away.

Plus, on Monday morning people will have a pretty good idea of what they are doing on Thursday, just a few days down the road. Many people have *no clue* what they will be up to in ten days. Furthermore, people like to see how their week will develop. People do not commit to things too far in advance. This is the reality of our culture today.

Ideally your meeting will happen in just a few days. If you must schedule it further out, do not extend invitations until the date is closer.

Here are the important elements to remember when planning your meeting:

1. A meeting should start promptly.
2. A meeting should be simple.
3. Distractions should be kept to a minimum.
4. A meeting should last no more than an hour.
5. Questions should be held until the end.
6. A meeting should be the same every time.
7. Shop talk should be kept to a minimum.

You should adhere to the above rules and pass them down as your business starts to grow.

Home Meeting Do's and Don'ts

Now let's cover a few do's and don'ts of your home meeting in more detail. This will prevent you from making some of the mistakes I made when I started out.

Do start your meeting on time, rather than delaying the meeting for that one special person about whom you are most excited. By delaying the start of your meeting you send the wrong message. Punctuality is vital on Venus. Making people wait is not professional or polite. It rewards people who arrived on time by making them sit around and wait for the guest who apparently matters more, even though they are late. Who would be open to a business offering presented with messages like that? Martians don't always consider the group as a whole. They forget to ask the important question, "What is in the best interest of everyone involved here right now?" It is critical to model considerate and thoughtful behavior for people in the room who may be joining your business down the road. Your future business partner may be one of the prompt people sitting on the couch. Remember network marketing is about duplication and people will copy you, so be a good role model.

Do keep your meeting simple and duplicable. I recommend having your front door ajar, which feels inviting to your guest as he walks toward your home. Having music on at a low volume can also make it more comfortable for the first guests to arrive. I suggest that you make water available. On Venus we serve water in a pitcher with real glasses. Venusians are aware that there are already too many plastic water bottles and cups on planet Earth. We must become environmentally responsible by limiting the amount of trash we generate.

You should make a few finger snacks available. Carrots, hummus, chips and salsa, cheese and crackers, or a vegetable tray with dip are inexpensive foods that are easy for guests to eat, and also easy for you to clean up afterward. In case you have a guest who is hungry, having come from work, you need to have something available for them to munch on. Pick snacks that your family likes, since we have a ton of no-shows in our line of work. You may be packing this stuff in your child's lunch tomorrow, so keep this in mind. The bottom line is that your new guest is watching. You want them to think, *"Wow, this is simple and inexpensive. I can definitely invite a few people to my home and do what she has done to get ready. I think I will do it."* When you set out to do something in your business, you must ask, "Can anyone in my business do what I just did?" If the answer is yes, then you are on the right track. But if the answer is no, you have gone off course and must get back on the path.

The occasional hostess will be flabbergasted when you suggest that she should not make Italian meatballs, artichoke dip, pizzas, and cannoli for dessert. She will shudder when you tell her not to serve red wine and vodka martinis. We all have our preferences and traditions. I have known a hostess to say that her friends would simply leave if she did not cook for them and serve alcohol. Though I generally believe this is too much and a possible distraction, I am not a stickler when it comes to the in-home event. I always share my thoughts about simplicity and duplication, and

I will attend a lavish meeting one time to see how it goes. I know what to expect, but I have been pleasantly surprised on a few occasions. The last thing I want to do is to alienate my new distributor. I will warn her that her guests may not feel as though they can duplicate what she is doing in the way of cooking and preparing for the event. However, if she is willing to give it a whirl one time, and she feels strongly about having food and drink available to her guests, I will go with the flow. I will also let her guests know that they will not have to pull out all the stops and host an in-home like the one they are attending if they decide to enroll in the business. I will compliment the hostess profusely but tell her friends that this is not representative of how we usually do these meetings. The hostess feels proud and appreciated, and in an ideal world the guests realize that they do not have to duplicate what she has done.

Do pay attention throughout the meeting. Take the time to turn off your phone in front of your guests, and invite them to mute theirs as well. Side conversations are taboo. It is distracting and rude to talk when other people are sharing in the front of the room. As the host, you need to pretend you have never before heard this information. Model excitement and interest and, believe me, the guests will follow suit. I do not care if you have seen your Company video ninety-two times. Pretend you are watching it for the first time, every time. To tell you the truth, I make it a game. I try to remember the very first time I watched my Company's video, and I challenge myself to get excited again and again. After all, watching that video literally changed my life. I want to be sure that every guest in the room has the opportunity to see the business the way I did. If you are whispering to your neighbor, checking text messages on your phone, or getting an iced tea in the kitchen, you are sending the wrong message. You are sending the message that "This is no big deal. You can check out, because it will be over soon." This is the last message you want your guests or anyone else's guests to receive. Remember—someday *you* will be the third-party validator at a meeting, and you may well need someone to validate for you at other meetings. Be courteous, not arrogant or self-centered. On Venus we truly work in partnership. We are gracious and open, friendly and helpful. Again, we know that a "rising tide raises all boats," and we are delighted to be of service.

Do plan ahead to minimize distractions before your guests arrive. It is crucial to get the kids, dogs, and cats situated before the meeting starts. Kids should not be running in and out of the meeting room, especially when the video is playing or the speaker is talking. Please use good common sense. Some people are afraid of dogs or allergic to cats, and children laughing and playing in the next room can be distracting. Do what you can to minimize noise and activity during the "body" of your meeting. Having kids and animals around *after* the presentation is not such a big deal. After all, we do this business so that we do not have to leave our families to go to work. Just be sensitive to the needs of the group.

Do invite your guests to hold questions until the end of the presentation. The main speaker has a presentation to deliver, and this can be a challenge in the best of times. If a guest has a question, invite her to find you after the meeting and ask her question personally, which will avoid wasting other people's time. Not everyone will be interested in the answer to this question. Another big reason for saving questions until the end is that once in a while, you will have a guest who has forgotten to leave his ego at the door. He may be skeptical, contentious, and even rude. It is best not to let him have the floor when you have no idea what is going to come out of his mouth. I am sure you have heard the phrase, "Don't let one bad apple spoil the whole bunch." Keep a tight rein on your meetings. You are the leader, and you can be polite and firm at the same time. Smile brightly when someone attempts to ask a question and say, "I'm excited to answer your question. Let's get together right after I finish my presentation so that we can talk. This way we will respect anyone who may need to leave at the end of the hour."

There is one more reason why questions should not be addressed during the presentation, and it may be the most important reason of all. I have mentioned several times that we are in the business of duplication. If you are constantly stopping to answer questions, the new distributor is never going to see a concise presentation from start to finish, and she will therefore be worried about a time in the future when she will be in front of the room. She may ask herself, *"How will I be able to field all of these questions efficiently? I don't want to look like a fool in front of a bunch of people. Maybe my doing a meeting isn't such a good idea."* This is the last thing you want her to decide. You want her to watch a presentation for the second or third time and say something like, *"I can do this. I will definitely be able to get up there and help with part of the presentation next time."* People want to feel relatively safe. If they see the same presentation again and again, they will start to feel more secure and confident in their own abilities. I promise!

Talk with a few of the distributors who are at your meeting before it starts and ask them if they are willing to share a one-to-two-minute business or product testimonial. This is group sponsoring at its finest. These "shares" should be very brief, with the goal of showing guests that the people seated next to them are friendly, smart, and just like them. This is third-party validation, and it works like a charm. If you invite two or three people to briefly share their story, it is likely that the guests in the room will relate to one or more of them. A story may inspire a guest to initiate a conversation and make a new friend after the presentation.

My takeaway for you is this: "Facts tell and stories sell." People are not half as interested in the features of your business as they are in the benefits. They want to know what the features are, but they *really* want to know, *"How is this feature going to change my life and get me out of pain?"* They may not even be aware that they want to know this. They may not know exactly what is causing their pain. A guest may be lonely and overwhelmed by raising children, feeling hugely disconnected from anything outside of playgroups and kindergarten. When a third-party validator talks about the travel, the incentives, and the events, a guest might start to wonder, *"Could this business provide fun, excitement, and connection for me while I'm raising my children?"*

You might have a guest who has recently divorced and is feeling rejected, sad, and broke. They may have attended the meeting just to get out of the house for a night. As they listen to a distributor talk about the death of his spouse and the fact that this business has provided a way for him to work from home, this guest may become quite interested in hearing more about the profession of network marketing. The bottom line is, people want to be able to *relate* to those people with whom they could potentially be working. It is your job, as the host or the presenter, to be sure that each guest feels safe and included. This is how we do it on Venus.

Here's another big no-no at home meetings, as well as in every other venue in which we gather in network marketing. Do not ask a lot of questions about a distributor's lineage at the in-home meeting. Asking things such as "Who is your upline?" or "Who got you into the business?" or "Are you in yet?" or "What rank are you?" is a bit nosy and can be off-putting, to say the least. Instead, ask questions like "Is this your first time attending an event?" or "Do you live in the area?" or "How did you come to attend the meeting tonight?" These questions are far more appropriate because they are less threatening. Additionally, distributors should limit the use of network marketing jargon in front of guests. Some network marketing lingo can really send up a red flag for a guest. Again, shop talk should be kept to a minimum when guests are in the vicinity; it's simply courteous.

Now let me share more about conducting the meeting.

CONDUCTING THE MEETING
The Welcome

The guests are seated, and you are starting on time. The kids are quiet and the animals are put away. Everyone has something to drink and a snack to keep them going for the next hour or so.

The new distributor gets up and welcomes people to his home. It goes like this: "Welcome to my home. I'm excited because..." This new person needs to be excited and passionate. Authenticity and enthusiasm are contagious. People cannot help but be drawn to you and your business idea if the time is right in their life!

We have talked about your story and how you will use it in creating connection with your prospects. When you are in front of the room welcoming your guests, you share an abbreviated version of your story. If you are excited about your products, share a bit about how you learned about them and what they have done to simplify or enhance your life. If you are passionate about the business model of network marketing and this is where your interest was strong, then share the details of how you learned about the opportunity, and what problems the business is solving or will potentially solve in your life. This "share" should last no more than two minutes and contain elements that everyone can relate to. Here is an example:

> I want to thank you all for coming tonight. I know
> you had a choice of where to spend your time, and

I'm grateful you have chosen to spend it here with us. I heard about XYZ Company just a few short months ago when Linda and I were working out together at the gym. I was sharing my frustrations about how fast the weekends go, and she mentioned that she works from home and that she has her own business. Well, I have worked my whole life for someone else, and I was intrigued and asked her to tell me more. The rest is history. We have been sharing this adventure ever since, and I am having fun for the first time in years. This is finally my opportunity to take my future into my own hands. I hope to earn enough income in the next six to twelve months so that I can quit my job and have more control over my life."

Here is another example:

Thank you for taking time out of your busy schedules to join me in my home to hear about my new business. I am so excited! I finally have the opportunity to determine what I am worth in the marketplace. Soon I will decide how much money I make and what hours I will work. More important, I will be able to decide what hours I will set aside for my family. I cannot wait to go to the bank when there is no line. I am excited about being able to go to the gym when there is no wait for the equipment. I know this business is going to give me back my freedom to choose.

Another example might go something like this:

Thank you for coming tonight my friends. I am grateful for your time and attention, and I promise to get you out of here within the hour. As I told some of you, I have known Greg for years. We went to college together, and he is seriously one of the smartest people I know. He was always known for being a "brain" in school. Greg and I ran into each other at the bank recently, and I said, "You sound so good! You look vital and fit. What are you doing differently, Greg?" That is when I heard about our products for the first time. I cannot believe how rested I feel after taking them. I am energized upon waking in the morning for the first time in years. After I experienced the results, I decided I wanted to share what I had discovered, and I joined the Company. I was not looking for something else to do but after learning about this, I just could not pass up the opportunity.

Whatever got your attention needs to be shared. Maybe it is the peace of mind you have received from signing up with a company that provides legal services. You might say something like "I cannot believe how secure I feel, knowing I have legal protection no matter what might come up in my life. What an incredible gift to my family and me."

This welcome needs to be short, concise, and interesting to everyone. You need to reiterate the fact that the meeting will be no more than an hour. The goal is to put your guests at ease and offer them the opportunity to sit back, relax, and enjoy the meeting. Remember: they are silently asking themselves, *"What's in it for me?"* This is Venus, and we are all about the people sitting in front of us. What are you offering that might enhance their lives and solve their problems? This is not the time to go on and on about your business background. This is not your opportunity to brag about your instant success with the Company and your plans for the future. A little dose of humility and encouragement will go a long way in gaining the respect and interest of the group. The goal is to open the minds of your guests. Your aim is to help them identify and connect with a place of longing that they may be feeling in their own lives. Ideally your products and business will serve as a means of alleviating some of their struggle.

INTRODUCE YOUR SPONSOR—
UPLINE OR THIRD-PARTY VALIDATOR

Again, your welcome should be short and informative. It is now time to introduce your sponsor or upline partner. It is important to let your friends and family know *why* they should listen to him or her. Be sure you have planned a strong introduction, even if it is not related to your partner's experience in network marketing. You followed him into the business, so you obviously have respect for him on some level. Be sure to share the details of why you admire and trust this person.

Here is an example:

> I've just gotten started with this Company, so I am still learning. I am excited to introduce my friend, colleague, and mentor, John Smith. John and I have worked together for a short time in this business, but I have known him for years. His kids go to school with ours, his wife is amazing, and he is an astute businessman and entrepreneur, avid marathon runner, and great father. He knows a lot more about this business than I do. I have asked him to share the Company story with you. John, I thank you for taking time away from your wife and kids to share some information with us.

John is the third-party validator we talked about in our discussion about the three-way call. Again, it is an essential and invaluable tool in building your network. People know and trust *you*, but they don't always *listen* to you. People are more likely to listen to the third-party validator as long as they know why they should listen, so be sure to do a good job in the introduction. Once again, proper planning is a key.

John says something like this:

> Wow, thank you for that kind introduction. I am very grateful to be here tonight, and excited to meet each and every one of you. Thank you for coming. I recognize that your time is valuable and I promise to be concise. I joined the Company about two years ago …

The third-party validator will spend no more than two minutes telling his or her story of how he or she joined your Company. Again, the details must be relatable. Each guest is listening and silently asking, *"What's in it for me?"*

THE PRESENTATION

Every good company has a business presentation that is shared at these in-home meetings. You will be taught the details of how to do it. The presentation usually includes a short, company-produced video that can be shown at the onset of the meeting by way of introduction or at the end of the meeting as a recap. Your sponsor will likely share the company story, the product story, the timing story, the compensation plan, and the details of how to get involved. This needs to take place in about thirty minutes, start to finish, without interruption. This is when the new distributors in the room need to be paying close attention and learning how to do the presentation in the future. This is duplication at its finest.

Here are a couple of subtler rules for the in-home meeting that make group sponsoring much more effective. First, it is always great to have four or five distributors attend the first in-home meeting, whether they are in your organization or not. These people are excited like you are. They know the details of the business and can answer questions and share their experiences and enthusiasm with the guests. Again, these are other voices with the same message. They will act as third-party validators when the scripted portion of the meeting is complete. Their energy will help carry the meeting as well as encourage and "lift" the speaker in the front of the room. This element of the home meeting cannot be overemphasized. Second, many times a new distributor will say something like "Well, I was planning to attend the meeting, but my guest canceled, so I just stayed home." When your guest cancels, it is disappointing. It is like moving your log farther away from the beach bonfire we talked about. You will have lost a bit of your own heat and enthusiasm. Skipping the meeting just moves the log a little farther away. When your guest cancels, you need the meeting. If you are already fired up and nothing can take away your fuel, the *meeting needs you*! If you want to be successful in network marketing, you will attend a minimum of two meetings per week. You need to have one of your own and attend someone else's. This is your business. Treat it as such. Commitment is doing what you said you would do long after the desire to do it has left you.

As we conclude our discussion of the home meeting, I want to highlight the two elements that need to be present in order to call it a success. They are the *call to action* and the *meeting after the meeting*.

THE CALL TO ACTION

After the thirty-minute scripted presentation and the few "shares" by the other distributors in the room, it's time to invite the guests to join the company. Honestly, I believe this one segment can either make or break the whole meeting. If the presentation was informative and authentic, the guests are likely to have a very good idea of how the business fits or might not fit into their life. If the timing is right for them, they are a "blue M&M," and they feel safe with you and the others, they will be primed and ready to listen intently to this section of your meeting. If they are interested in using your Company's products, they will be ready to hear the details of how to get them. If they are not interested in any of your offerings, they will be ready to chat with the other guests or get back to their homes and families. It is time to make a clear offer to everyone in the room and wrap the meeting. It needs to sound something like this:

I want to thank you for your attention during the presentation. Also, I would like to thank our hostess, Gina, for opening her home to us tonight. I have really enjoyed my time with all of you. I imagine that you are finding yourself in one of three categories tonight. You may be saying, *"Thanks for the information. I would like to do a little homework and I will be in touch."* We are delighted you came, and we are happy with that. (Venusians do not feel the need to push.)

You may be saying, *"Wow! Those products sound incredible! How much are they, and how can I get the best possible price?"* We can help you get your order placed tonight. [Have paper applications and computers available to get it done.]

If you are like me, you are chomping at the bit to know, *"How can I get these products for myself and share them with others? How can I create passive, residual income? How much is it going to cost me to get started right now, and how fast can I get a return on my investment?"*

I am going to make it clear, simple, and concise so you can get back to your families if you need to or hang around if you would like to get your questions answered. If you must leave right away please do me a favor. If you would let Gina know what your intentions are while you're on your way out, I

would be really grateful. Let her know you are going to take time to check it out, you are interested in
becoming a customer, or you would like to join our
team. Then we will not have to wonder.

THE MEETING AFTER THE MEETING

The presenter will then do a quick rundown of the options and
close the meeting. This is the end of the official presentation and
the beginning of the meeting after the meeting. This is the most
important part of the evening. It is time for the guests to ask questions and bond with the other distributors in the room. As the host
or presenter, you will take this time to make a quick sweep of the
room to find out who is going to take you up on any of your offerings.

If everyone runs out of the house right after you finish the
presentation, it means one of two things: either your hygiene is in
question or you went on too long. My guess is that it's the latter.
The in-home presentation is a brief overview, not a deep study. Do
not try to share every detail at the meeting. In our profession we
refer to this as throwing up on the prospect. It is a distasteful analogy on purpose. If you can remember it, you are less likely to do it
to your potential distributors.

I encourage people to be direct and soft in their approach after
the meeting, perhaps asking a question like "What did you like
most about tonight?" or "What grabbed your attention tonight?"
or "How do you see yourself getting involved with our Company?"

If they do not see themselves getting involved, they will tell you, and that is good. Do not be afraid of getting a no. In our world, every no brings us closer to a yes. To put it another way, if you are not getting any no's, then you are certainly not getting any yeses. You cannot have one without the other.

One more thing before I move on: do *not* let anyone leave your meeting without a takeaway from your Company. It could be a company CD or DVD. It could be a magazine, brochure, or company newsletter. Remember—if you are a distributor attending the meeting as a guest or with a guest, you will provide any materials that you give out. It is not up to the hostess to supply materials to other teams and their guests. We each pay for this stuff. Remember to be courteous and gracious by being prepared with your own supplies.

Before your guest leaves, you might write a few website links on a piece of paper or use a computer and send them some e-mails right then and there. Remember people do not want to be pushed, but they definitely want to be skillfully led. If they are considering the opportunity, they are asking themselves, *"Will I be able to do what she's doing if I join these people?"* Everything you do is noted. Every step of the way your guest is deciding if they can duplicate your actions. It's a huge responsibility. Once again, you must be bad before you are good and good before you are great. Use your sponsor, upline partner, or sideline friend to help you answer questions and move the prospect to make a decision.

It really is a wonderful business. When I help you get what you want, I get what I want; lovely. Venus. Pay it forward. Love enough people, and you will create a business that will give back for years and even decades to come.

The Magic of Scripts

I have talked about some very useful power tools that are used to build a solid network marketing business. Your story is a huge opportunity to connect with your new prospect. The three-way call is an effective way to facilitate a relationship between your prospect and another person inside your Company. The three-way call allows this potential business partner to hear the same story from a different perspective. These tools are *powerful*. When used correctly, they can be extremely effective in helping you attract people to your business. Another power tool that will aid in building your business is using scripted training. This is a way to leverage the power of duplication and to provide the safe environment for your new distributor to put down their roots and grow. I am going to share how I came to know the importance of using scripts; to do so I must go back thirty years when I was in my twenties.

I'm recalling the time I was forced to get my first "real" job. I had waited tables, bartended, and taught fitness classes all through college and for a few years afterward. I was in a rut. It was definitely time to make a change, but I had no idea what I wanted to do. I only knew what I did not want to do. One day I fell at work and pulled a quad muscle. I was instantly unemployed. I could not walk, and I certainly could not jump. The doctor said, "No waiting tables and no teaching." My income disappeared overnight.

I have amazing parents, but I did not call them. I had been out of the house for years, and I was not going to bother them for money. I grabbed the classifieds. I responded to an ad that said something like "Do you love kids? Do you love to read? If you answered yes to both of these questions, call the number below for a phone interview. Only serious people should apply." I was serious. I responded to the ad, and an interview was scheduled for the very next day.

There were about fifty other applicants, and one by one we were called into a little room. I think I got about ten minutes with the interviewer, and I told him I was passionate, enthusiastic, and hungry for the job. I did not care what it was. I needed it. He told me he would call only the people he was interested in the next day. I do not know if I have ever been happier to receive a phone call in my life. I got the job that changed the course of my life forever.

On Monday morning thirty of us showed up for the job. It turned out to be door-to-door encyclopedia sales. I looked to the left and right of me. These people were of high caliber, and they were motivated like I was. I decided right then and there that I would be the very best salesperson in the group. I could not afford to lose this job, and I was going to work like I had never worked before to rise to the top of this new company.

One of the first things my new boss did was pass out a written script. He then put us through a scripted training on how to sell this series of books. It was a lot to memorize, and we had only one day. I watched him like a hawk and took notes. Before we left he had us sit in a room and listen to one-hour audiotapes: one by Napoleon Hill, author of *Think and Grow Rich,* and one by the legendary Zig Ziglar. I had no idea who these men were, but their words seared my heart and soul. They talked about the 80/20 rule in sales. They said that 80 percent of the people do 20 percent of the work and 20 percent of the people do 80 percent. Then they talked about the 1-percenters. These were the super-achievers— the cream of the crop. I yearned to be one of them. I ached to be successful. I knew in my heart that I was one of them. I hung on to every word and practically ran out of the room to learn the script.

I spent hours that night committing every single word to memory. It was a ton of work, but I had no safety net. I had to succeed. I had to stand out. I had to be the best of the bunch. The following day I walked into the room well dressed and confident. When my boss asked for a volunteer, my hand shot up without hesitation. It startled me when I looked right and left and saw that mine was the only hand in the air. I went to the front of the room and ran through the script. It was a little bumpy, but I did it. People were blown away, and he could not get anyone else to volunteer. I was shocked. Who does not do their homework? I could hardly believe the other people had not prepared. It took me years and years to figure out that most people just do not follow through. Something stops them from doing what they say they will do. My boss gave us another script, and we listened to more audiotapes before leaving the building. The words of Denis Waitley and Tom Hopkins sparked my passion for memorizing more scripts. I showed up the next day totally ready. A third of the room was empty. Instead of thirty people there were just twenty. It did not faze me.

The next day I drove an hour from Huntington Beach to San Clemente to knock on doors and share the concept of reading with the people who lived behind them. I asked questions. I was beyond nervous. I was terrified. I shared statistics about the importance of reading with children. I opened each of the posters and used my scripted training to share the books. I gave my customers the payment options and asked for the sale just the way I had been taught. I used additional scripts to handle at least four objections, because I learned that most sales take place after the fourth or fifth no. I used courage and belief to transform my fear into fearlessness. I was awful, and then I was bad. I was bad, and then I was good. I finally went from good to great because I repeated the same words again and again and *made them mine.*

I made $27,000 in eight months with that company. I was the last person standing. Everyone else quit. Every single day before we went out to sell, we listened to audiotapes. I loved listening to Jim Rohn and John Maxwell and was fortified by their messages of inspiration and hope.

The experience I gained selling books door-to-door in my midtwenties was invaluable. It was boot camp, and it set me up for the success I experienced more than two decades later. One of my biggest takeaways was the importance and value of using scripted training. I never would have had the confidence to walk into the home of complete strangers, and attempt to make a $1,695 sale if I had not had the exact road map and precise training. Armed with the "system," I was able to excel.

In everything I have done since selling books in the late eighties, I have either used scripted training that was provided to me or developed it myself. When I sold temporary-help services, I devoured their training. When I sold home décor items, I wrote scripts and shared them with my group. I have never been comfortable winging it, and I do not believe others are comfortable winging it either.

You might think, "I am uncomfortable using other people's words." You may say, "It does not feel authentic to memorize a script and recite it." I can certainly understand how you might feel this way. I urge you to memorize the script anyway and practice, practice, practice. With time, it will become more and more familiar to you. The longer you work with it, the closer you will be to "owning it." If there is a line or a way of expressing an idea that does not resonate with you, then change it. If there are some words that just do not sound like you, then remove them and replace them with words that feel more comfortable. Be cautious, though. If a script has been written and used successfully by other people who have come before you, then do not change it too much. Sometimes each word has been chosen on purpose. A script is often carefully crafted to elicit a desired emotion or response. If you trust the people or the system you are following, then learn it to the letter until you have a good reason to change it. This is part of being an excellent student. Excellent students do their homework. Memorizing scripts is important when you are new. It gives you a well-proven track to run on. Even more important, it gives your people tracks as well.

Follow Up and Close

If you've been in network marketing or most any other business, you have heard, "The fortune is in the follow-up." This is doubly true for network marketing. Nothing is more important than the concept of following up and following *through*. It has taken me years to understand that most people just do not do it. Sadly, people genuinely struggle with the basic principle "Do what you *say* you will do."

When I participated in a personal development seminar called Landmark Education, I was relatively young and quite new to the business world. I will never forget a specific hour of the course when the instructor, sitting on a stool on stage, began to discuss the concept of follow-through. His calm beginning quickly escalated into a full-blown rant. He was quite heated and shouted things like "You people do not return phone calls. You do not finish what you have started! You do not follow up and you do not follow through! And you wonder why you are failing your way through life!" What blew my mind was how fast I heard people begin to sniff and pull out the Kleenex. Soon the cacophony was in full swing, and the sobbing and snorting and painful wailing were all around me. I silently wondered if someone had been shot. I realized that the seminar participants were identifying with his accusations. People were embarrassed, feeling guilty, and mortified by their lack of commitment to themselves. Their pain was real, authentic, and raw. The instructor continued to rail at us about our lack of commitment to others and about the fact that we were short on tenacity and perseverance. He urged us to remember all the times we had quit on ourselves.

I was looking down, but my eyes were wide open. I absolutely could not relate. I did not have a long history in business, but I assure you my parents taught me about following up, following through, and honoring my commitments. My mom and dad did not fall short in this area and neither did I. I sensed that I was one of the very few attendees who could not relate to his accusations. The others were deeply remorseful and wading through their pain. I kept my head down, for the most part. Eventually, though, I just had to look up at the instructor. We locked eyes. He urged me to cry. He wanted me to admit to *own* my lazy ways. He was determined to break me. If I could have caved, I would gladly have done so. That's just the kind of people pleaser I was back then. But I could not make it happen. He was barking up the wrong tree. In this regard, I was clean and clear, and I was not remotely close to cracking. I stared him down and owned my innocence that day. That is also the day I became aware that most people struggle in this area. Most people do not follow up or follow through. They do not do what they say they will do. It is a form of self-sabotage that will destroy you and your network marketing business. Get a life coach, get real, or get out. If you do not get over this hurdle, you will not be successful in this business. It's as simple as that. Sometimes brutal honesty is required on Venus.

In his book *Go Pro*, Eric Worre (2013) says, "The only reason to have an exposure is to set up the next exposure." He goes on to remind us, "It takes four to six exposures for the average person to join network marketing." I am in 100 percent agreement. Very few people will see your presentation and respond with "Wow, awesome! Sign me up!" You will need to learn to be patient. You are like a farmer planting seeds. How crazy would it be to plant a tomato seed today and step into the garden tomorrow saying, "Where are my tomatoes? I planted the seed yesterday! I'm hungry. I guess this plant just is not going to grow."

You may laugh when I use this analogy, but some of you expect people to jump wildly into your business and run like the wind to make you rich. This is a naive and self-serving way of approaching our profession. Furthermore it contributes to the negative view of network marketing that I am so passionate about changing.

On the first exposure, most people will listen to your presentation in a skeptical way or at a minimum, passively sit there in WIIFM mode (What's in It for Me?). If you are doing your job, they will walk away with a website, a DVD, an audio CD, or a magazine that will serve to corroborate the details you have shared with them. Their review of these materials will serve as exposure number two.

As I have mentioned before, we do three things in the business of network marketing. We expose people to our business idea, we promote from event to event, and we build community. It is important to be plugged in to the business - and community-building events that are taking place all over your area and beyond. If you are learning the business of network marketing, you will ask for a follow-up conversation and exposure number three. To do that efficiently, you will need to know when the next meeting is taking place in your prospect's area or the details of the next big event. Your job is to become extremely proficient at using polite persistence and third-party validation in familiarizing your potential business partner with the culture and business practices of your network marketing company. Using the concept of group sponsoring will be critical to your success and to the success of your business partners.

The language you use and the confidence around follow-up is critical as well. For example, as a new distributor you might be tentative about asking questions after the three-way call, the one-on-one meeting, the two-on-one, or the in-home presentation. You might timidly ask, "So, what do you think? Do you want to sign up?" Who would want to follow someone so wishy-washy and weak? Some people don't say anything more than "Thanks for taking a look. Let me know if you have any questions" and they are done. New distributors are often afraid of coming on too strong. They are nervous and it shows. They lack conviction in what they are doing. There is a safe way to strike the right balance between a strong posture and allowing a prospect the space to move through the process at a pace that suits them. It's called *authenticity*. Be real. Communicate fully. Share your feelings, and it will give other people permission to do the same.

Sharing authentically, you will summarize your feelings about the time you have spent together. It should sound something like this:

Jim, I really appreciate you taking the time to check out the Company. I know you are busy. As I said earlier, I would be honored to have you join me in this business.

You will then follow with a closing question, which will be a barometer question. The answer to this temperature taker will give you some idea of their interest level. It needs to be a question that requires more than just a yes or no answer. Here are some examples:

- I'm curious: What did you like best about what you heard tonight?
- I wonder—how do you see yourself getting involved with this company?
- What questions do you have after hearing the presentation?
- How would you like me to proceed with you?
- Is this something you would like to hear more about?
- Do you see how this might help you get your free time back in the next two to five years?
- On a scale from one to ten—one being not interested at all and ten being "sign me up right now"—where do you see yourself?" (If they answer, "I am a five," be sure to ask, "Why didn't you say you are a four?")

Asking a closing question is critical to uncovering your prospect's concerns. They will respect you for openly and authentically asking them where they stand after hearing your presentation. Remember that you cannot answer a question that is not asked. Similarly, you cannot flush out a concern that is never identified and expressed.

On Venus, we are not afraid to communicate fully and completely. We know that we will never earn the respect of our potential business partners if we do not establish trust and create open lines of communication from the beginning of our business relationships. We are fearless in our quest for like-minded entrepreneurs who want to make a difference in the lives of others. It's a huge responsibility to take on a new distributor. We recognize the enormity of the commitment we have made when we do so, and are not afraid to handle the objections, hesitations, and fears that come up as our potential business partners get closer and closer to joining us.

One last point about follow-up before we move on: it is imperative that we check back with our prospects every thirty to forty-five days. I say something like this:

> Linda, I thank you for listening to me today. I respect and appreciate your telling me the timing just is not quite right for you now. I know your job is busy and that you are consumed with your big project and kids at the moment. I do believe you will hear about these products from other people in the

future. I also believe you may hear about the opportunity that we discussed today. I want to ask you
for two favors.

She just told you "no", so she will want to support you.

First, I want to ask you if it is okay if I stay in touch
with you and keep you apprised of my progress. I
would love to keep you up to date and let you know
how I am doing. [Wait for the person to commit by
saying yes.] Second, I just want you to remember
that I am the person who has brought these products and the business offering to your attention. If
someone else shares it in the next few months, just
remember you heard it from me first. Again, I admire and respect you so much. It would be an honor
to have you in my business sometime in the future.

Again, you just follow up with your prospects. You have taken
the time to reach out and share what you have. As I mentioned
before, people usually do not say yes the very first time they hear
about your business. Be efficient. Be professional. Ask for permission to keep in touch, and *do it*. Situations change. People change.
Life happens. What is not of interest today may be of extreme interest in as little as thirty, sixty, or ninety days. Network marketing
professionals know the power of building trust and relationships

over time. If you keep notes and follow up consistently and effectively with genuine concern, you will draw people to you with your courteous and persistent professionalism. You may be the very first person your prospect thinks of when change comes knocking at their door. If *you* do not follow up, someone else will. That is a fact. It is true. The fortune really is found in the follow-up!

10

MORE USEFUL STUFF

HANDLING OBJECTIONS

IN SALES, AND FROM MARS, we hear about handling objections as if they are enemies that must be defeated in order to
win. Venusians do not worry about so-called objections. In fact, if
we have a lay-down (someone who says yes immediately, without
hesitation), it is probably a bit more concerning. For example, the
prospect who is extremely impulsive and says yes to everything
may not understand the concept of actually building a business. If
your prospect is taking the time to ask questions, get clarification,
and express concern, you should be delighted. You may have a
blue M&M!

How you handle the concerns of your prospect may positively
differentiate you from anyone with whom he has come into con-

tact before. Responding to an objection may also be your very first opportunity to gain insight and build trust with your potential business partner. The best advice I can give is to remember that God gave us two ears and one mouth. Listening to what is being said and identifying some of what is not being said is central to learning more about what makes your prospect tick. If you end up building a business together, this information will be invaluable to you. Be attentive and listen with an open mind. Leave your head and use your heart when your prospect is vulnerable enough to offer more than "Let me take this home and look it over. I'll get back to you."

It is important to ask an open-ended closing question—one that will encourage your prospect to think and will elicit more than a simple yes or no. Ask your question and be prepared to wait and listen. After all, *you* knew what you were going to ask, but your prospect did not. He may need time to process your question, decide how he is going to respond, formulate his answer, and figure out how to share it with you. He may also be having an inner battle while trying to decide if he will open up to you with his concerns. Your only job at this point is to ask the question, sit back, and breathe. Learn to get comfortable with the silence. Get comfortable with the GAP (God's Area of Preparation) in the conversation.

You may struggle with this pregnant pause. I know I did. Years ago I would ask the question, wait a second or two, and go right back to selling because I could not bear the silence. I would continue to share more features and benefits so I would not have to experience the angst that my closing question was causing me. I was nervous, which likely made my prospect uncomfortable as well. I forgot for the moment that the conversation was not about me. It was about him or her.

Eventually I developed a system that I still use today. I ask the closing question and immediately retreat to my nonattached place. I imagine myself with Gordon and the kids at the beach or in San Clemente at my favorite restaurant with my mom, or walking my dog, Cash with Gordon on a mild, sunny day. It gives me a sense of calm and control and allows my prospect the time and the space to consider the question I have posed. This works for me, and I hope it helps you too. Giving your potential distributor/business partner a few minutes to wrestle with their fears and insecurities is essential. If you give them time to drop from their head and into their heart, they will be more likely to give you the real concern and not just the first one that pops into their mind, such as "I'd love to join you, but money's tight right now."

People will tell you all day long that they do not have the money. My advice? Do not believe them, because most of the time it is not true: seriously. Whether or not your prospect actually *has* the money available in his checking account is irrelevant. In fact, if your prospect *does* have the money readily available and immediately purchases the starter kit or your Company's package, there may be little or no commitment to actually working the business. The purchase is only one step closer to engagement. It is not a guarantee. They may be excited to get your products and use them and that is all. Conversely, squirming, pondering, restless prospects may be asking themselves the real question, sometimes the only question—the question that may plague them for days, weeks, months, or even years: *"Can I really do this?"* Let's face it. Most people do not come out and say, "I am really wondering whether I have what it takes to be successful. I have failed before, and I don't want to fail again."

Since I know this to be true, I am going to share the common decoy questions that come up on the journey to the real concern. I will teach you how to isolate the initial objection, how to handle it, and how to uncover the big daddy of them all, which is "Can I do this?" If you do not uncover it, you cannot handle and dissipate it.

As I have mentioned before, network marketing is a simple business; it just is not easy. Most of the questions you ever get will surface in the first ninety days of building your business. Your prospect may bring up one or more of these concerns. Your job is to deal with them one by one as if you have never heard them before.

When your prospect is sharing, the last thing you want to do is nod as though you have heard it all before and just cannot wait for them to be finished so you pacify them with one of your canned answers (That would be the Mars mentality.) Nobody wants to be treated this way. You may not need to hear the rest of the question to answer it, but they definitely need the time and space to ask it. Everyone deserves to be *heard*. Listening with interest as if you are hearing it for the first time is critical to building trust. Be patient and let them ask their question completely. You have taken the time to set the appointment, to meet with them, and to share your products and opportunity. Now take the time to finish the appointment with respect. Listen to what they are saying and be present to what they may not be expressing. Pay attention to their body language and tone of voice. It will tell you a lot about where they are coming from.

Remember—objections are just requests for more information. They can also be used as stall tactics. Your prospect may need some time to process information, gather more, and refer to previous experiences to determine how to proceed in a way that will create a win-win for you and for them.

Here are the common objections you will hear as your prospect gets closer to decision-making time.

FIVE COMMON OBJECTIONS IN NETWORK MARKETING

1. I am not a salesperson.
2. I don't have time to do this business.
3. Is this multilevel marketing?
4. Is this market saturated?
5. I don't have the money.

I will address each one individually. I will acknowledge, clarify, restate, ask a question, isolate, and answer them to the best of my ability. When you are in front of a prospect, do not leave out any of the steps mentioned above. The time spent is about really hearing your prospect. It is about figuring out how their mind works. It is about learning what they believe. This information is critical in helping them move forward if the timing is right for them and for *you*. Again, taking someone on is serious business. When your prospect tells you yes and becomes a distributor/business partner, the work of helping them succeed has just begun.

We are about to get back to scripted training. I absolutely believe it is important, but it is no substitute for genuine connection. If your prospect does not feel heard and understood, no memorized script is going to move them to act. Please remember this as you read the ideas below.

1. I'M NOT A SALESPERSON.

Acknowledge, Clarify, Restate, and Ask a Question

> Jill, I really appreciate your willingness to share your concern with me. I want to make sure I have understood you correctly. I hear you saying that you are not comfortable with selling. It sounds to me like you believe you would need to have a good background in sales to be successful in network marketing. Is that right?

Who would not feel heard if you approached every hesitation in this way? And if for some reason you have not gotten it just right, this method of clarification allows the prospect the freedom to give you more information about what is holding them back.

Isolate

> Jill, I thank you again for opening up to me today. I really hear you when you tell me that selling is not something you feel comfortable doing, and I can appreciate that. I really don't see myself as a salesperson either. Let me ask you this: If I can show you how I build my network marketing business without selling, would you be interested in moving forward with me? In other words, is this the only thing you are struggling with, or is there something else that might stop you from joining my team?

At this point Jill might tell you she is also concerned about what others will think about her since she has tried network marketing in the past and it has not worked for her. As long as you are tuned in and empathetic, the objections will get more and more personal as the conversation continues. The real objection will not always be the first one put forth by your prospect. Answer the one at hand, and continue to isolate and answer until you feel that you are dealing with the hesitation that is really stopping them.

Answer

> Honestly, Jill, I do not think most people in network marketing see themselves as salespeople. I know I

don't. I believe we are sharing products that have meaning and value for us. It is natural to share something you love. When I read a good book, I buy a few copies and give them away. I cannot help it! When you go to a great restaurant or movie don't you just feel compelled to tell other people about it? [Look for agreement.] When my friends tell me they hate their job or are frustrated by their boss or how they have always dreamed of having their own business, I feel like I would be neglecting them if I did not share what I know.

If you are tuned in to the conversation, you will be able to answer this objection with ease and grace. Use empathy and listen to your prospect. They will feel heard and appreciated, and will likely share even more with you.

2. I DON'T HAVE TIME TO DO THIS BUSINESS.

Acknowledge, Clarify, Restate, and Ask a Question

Ron, I am so grateful that you would feel safe enough with me to share this concern. I want to be sure I really understand where you are coming from. You mentioned that you are very busy with real estate and your family, and I really heard you. I am guessing that you do not really feel you can take advantage of this business opportunity because of the fact that there are not enough hours in the day. Let me ask you this: How much time do you think you will need to devote to your network marketing business to be successful?

Asking this question is going to tell you a lot about Ron's work ethic and his expectations. He may think he has to quit his job to join you. If you do not ask, you may never know what he is thinking about the time requirement. You may lose a hot one just because you did not flush out the concern.

Isolate

Wow, I'm really glad I asked this question, Ron. I totally understand that you have a huge need for security since you have three kids and a wife to look after. Thank you for expressing how much you love and care for each of them. You are a wonderful father and husband. Let me ask you this: If I could show you a way to build this business and still work full-time in real estate, would you want to hear more? I mean, is there anything else that is stopping you from moving forward, or is it really just the time commitment that is concerning you?

Now listen closely to his answer to ensure you are getting his full message.

Answer

> Ron, you are not alone. Most people get excited when they see the potential for residual income that our Company offers. Like you, they assume they would have to quit their job to take advantage of this opportunity. Although lots of people might like to walk away from their full-time job, most are not able to do so for financial reasons. If I can show you how thousands of people have worked for two to five years about ten hours per week to obtain financial and time freedom with my Company, would that interest you?

3. IS THIS MULTILEVEL MARKETING?

Ask a Question

> Yes it is! Tell me what you know about
> network marketing, Gina.

Until you gain understanding, there is nothing to acknowledge, clarify, or restate. Just don't assume that network marketing is a problem for your prospect. Be ready to hear something like

"Awesome! I love network marketing" because our profession is coming of age. People are recognizing that a good network can be an answer to their prayers. Be positive about our business model. Your measured enthusiasm will not go unnoticed. It's contagious. Be confident, and have fun talking about a profession that you can be proud of.

Unfortunately, your prospect may have preconceived notions about what network marketing is and what it is not. In addition, she may have had a personal experience in the past that left her frustrated and bitter. Remember your job is to listen with interest and invite her to share her experience with you. It's much easier to answer an objection if you have a keen understanding of what the objection is. She may not know much at all about networking and may ask this similar question:

"Is it one of those pyramid schemes?"

Acknowledge and Clarify

> Gina, I am so glad you brought this up so we can talk about it. Can you tell me exactly what you mean by a pyramid scheme? I just need to understand where you are coming from.

She will likely get a little flustered and answer with something like this:

You know—one of those things where you get in and get your friends in and the people at the top make all the money.

Or this:

Well, I have to be honest. I do not know much about them, but my sister tried one once and she did not make any money at all and drove us all crazy trying to sell us her products.

The chances are good that your potential business partner is getting a bit embarrassed and feeling quite uneducated about what you do. They may even become apologetic if you let them ramble long enough. For this very reason it is important to let them fully express their concerns. They may admit that they really know very little about what you do. They may become more open-minded and want to obtain a clearer understanding. This is where your calm excitement comes in.

Isolate

Gina, it sounds to me like you really need to understand the difference between an illegal pyramid and a legitimate network marketing business before you can move forward. If I can show you that our Company is not only legal, but also legitimate and ethical, is there anything else that would stop you from joining me as a business partner today?

Answer

Again, Gina, I am really grateful you shared your concern. I am glad we can talk about it openly, so I can tell you what I have learned about this profession and why it excites me so much. There are reasons why people sometimes get a jaded view of network marketing, and I want you to have a clear understanding of how and why this happens in our business. It will help you should you decide to work with me.

First, though, I want to talk about that "pyramid scheme". Pyramid schemes are nothing more than money games, and they are illegal. It is an exchange of money among friends. There is no product involved. We have an incredible product line, and we are members of the Direct Selling Association. The DSA is the watchdog for our profession, and most reputable companies are card-carrying members.

I think the reason so many people have a jaded view of network marketing is that the barrier to entry is so low. Anyone who wants to try their hand at network marketing can do so because it costs so little to get in.

When people buy a franchise like MacDonald's, for instance, it costs them literally millions. There is huge risk and a big commitment when people spend the money and time to do the research, purchase the franchise, and go through the training to be successful.

When people sign up with network marketing companies, their commitment level may be very low. Since people can join for so little, it's hard for them to imagine the huge upside potential that is actually available. Honestly, it is like anything else: You get out of it what you put into it. If you treat it like a hobby, it will pay you like one. If you treat it like the multimillion-dollar business it can become and do it consistently over time, it may well pay you for the rest of your life. People do not always understand this when they pay their money and join the Company. Often they will make a few calls after little training, get shot down, and then say they are done. When someone mentions network marketing down the road, they flippantly say, "I tried that once. It did not work for me." I really encourage you to take the time to learn about the profession. I think you will be pleasantly surprised when you take a closer look.

Have fun answering people's questions, and ask for what you want. Let them know that you are excited about the idea of working with them. Do not be afraid to ask them to join you right then and there. If you are authentic, they will likely feel comfortable enough to ask you if they have more questions.

4. IS THIS MARKET SATURATED?

Ask a Question

Don, I want to do a good job answering your question. May I ask what you mean by "saturated"?

Acknowledge, Clarify, Restate, and Isolate

You know, Don, I'm really glad you brought up that concern. I can see it is important to you, and I want you to be confident that this opportunity will be a good one for you and for those people who join you in the future. If you feel confident that this business will be viable for years to come, would you feel comfortable moving forward with me? [Listen for acknowledgment.] Is there anything else that is holding you back from getting started?

Answer

Your question is a good one. In real estate it is location, location, location. In network marketing it is timing, timing, timing! Good for you for asking about the timing of our Company. Here is how I see it. You have told me you are excited about our products and that you had not heard of them. You also mentioned that your sister and mother have not either. Until everyone on your street is using our products or has heard of them and made a decision not to use them, the opportunity is viable. In addition, the timing just could not be better for our profession. People are sick and tired of being sick and tired, and are increasingly interested in working for themselves and controlling their own time. They are tired of being told when they will work, when they will vacation and what they are worth in the marketplace. People are looking for options.

There is a book called The Next Millionaires (2006), by *New York Times* best-selling author Paul Zane Pilzer. He talks about a vast amount of new wealth that is being created in network marketing, and how people can "shrug off the pessimism and malaise of the times and grasp and ride the surging currents of new wealth creation to become the next millionaires."

Let's lock arms, work this business together and take control of our lives, shall we?

5. I DON'T HAVE THE MONEY.

Acknowledge, Clarify, Restate, and Ask a Question

So let me see if I have this right, Juanita. You're excited about the products and about the business. You believe you could find the time to do this and that you can be successful at it. If we could come up with a creative way to find the money, would you be all in right now?

Isolate

Is there anything else stopping you or is it just the financial piece?

Answer

The answer to this objection will vary from situation to situation. As I mentioned earlier, people perceive that they do not have the money until it becomes a priority for them. I have used the "I do not have the money" excuse plenty of times in my life because it was easier than saying, "I am not ready to commit to spending money on what you are offering." Please remember this when your prospect says, "I would like to join, but I really cannot afford it." This is why isolating the objection is so important. The big one is often lurking behind the money one. Your prospect may be secretly wondering, *"Do I really have what it takes to be successful in network marketing?"*

THE "FEEL, FELT, FOUND" TECHNIQUE

The feel, felt, found technique seems a little canned at first glance, but it is extremely effective and has become second nature to me now that I've used it for decades. I have even used it in raising my boys or counseling a friend. People have used it on me, and I have recognized and even appreciated it. Let's take a look.

Barbara, I know how you feel. I've been in this business for a long time and constantly sit down with people who are struggling to make ends meet. It seems that there is always too much month at the end of their money. Every time they get ahead, it seems like another bill pops up and the money is suddenly spoken for. It is always something: new tires, dental work, or kids' braces. You name it, I have heard it.

After being around for a while, I have found that there is never the perfect time when the money is just 'sitting around' without a home. I would really like to help you change your situation. I would like to help you create some residual income so you do not have to live from check to check. If you find a way to get started now, I will work like crazy to get your return on investment as fast as possible. Shall we do this together?

If I know someone quite well, I have been known to say something like this:

Chuck, come on. You are a bartender and a UPS delivery guy. If you are out with your kids and someone slashes your tires at the restaurant, you still have to get to work tomorrow, right? You would have to come up with the money to get four tires on your car so you could get to work. I'm talking about changing your financial future forever. I honestly believe with all my heart that we can do this together. Can you figure out a way to get started so we can create a different financial reality for you in the future? Is there anything else that you are not sharing with me that would keep you from taking the plunge?

I have been in this business for a long time and have found that where there is a will, there is a way. Truly. I have seen families clean out their homes and have garage sales. I have seen people take a loan against their 401(k)s, not that I recommend that. I have seen people sell motorcycles, guitars, and stamp collections to join network marketing. I have even heard of a guy digging a tree out of his front yard and selling it to get involved in this profession.

You do not know what is burning inside a person. You cannot necessarily see the passion they have for finding a way to join you. If they want it, they will get the money. It is as simple as that. Sometimes calling them out helps force them to get real with you and with themselves. They may finally admit they are scared. They may tell you they have failed in the past and are afraid of failing again. They may share that they have an unsupportive spouse at home. They may tell you they just got laid off and are scared to death to spend the money they have allotted for rent.

An extremely successful person may be struggling with a whole different array of concerns. Maybe they are afraid of looking like they have failed in their current business because they have joined your network. Maybe they need help formulating their story so it is moving and effective without making them look like a failure. Your prospect may wonder how he is going to tell people he is a real estate agent by day and a network marketer by night.

The only way to know what another person is thinking is to ask them. Be respectful and patient. Be empathetic and listen well. We are not interested in "getting one" on Venus. We are extremely interested in lightening the load of the person who walks beside us. Zig Ziglar reminds us, "You can have everything in life you want, if you will just help other people get what they want."

Objections are awesome. Objections are a huge part of connecting with others and building relationships. Become a professional at handling objections because you care and because you are authentic in your desire to help people. If you combine this skill with a tremendous work ethic, staying power, and tenacity, your success in network marketing is strengthened.

THE CLOSE REVISITED

I briefly covered "the close" in a previous chapter on follow-up. Because most people do not join network marketing after hearing about it just one time, I think it is vitally important to share more detail about the close and how important I believe it to be.

In this discussion, I will start by referencing Roger Clarke's "diffusion of innovation" theory. His theory is concerned with the manner in which a new technological idea, artifact, or technique, or a new use of an old one, migrates from creation to use. Roger's theory concludes that only 16 percent of individuals in a social system qualify as "innovators" or "early adopters". These are people who see a new idea and adopt it immediately. Another 68 percent are considered to be somewhere in the middle of the bell curve and qualify as the "early majority" and the "late majority". The last 16 percent are called "laggards". These folks are the very *last* people to jump on board. They are skeptical and slow to pull the trigger. I am a "laggard" when it comes to technology. I got my first iPhone many years after the original model came on the scene. Also, it was many years before I used the search engine Google when I came upon a word I didn't know. I was using a printed dictionary and thesaurus long after most people had donated theirs to the used bookstore. I have always been a "laggard" when it comes to computers, electronics, and phones.

Although I am quite slow in adopting new ideas in some areas of my life, I am extremely quick when it comes to new information about health and network marketing. I have been lucky enough to see around corners in these areas. When I joined my first network I thought, *"Wow, why would anyone ever say no to a business like this? Who wouldn't be interested in residual income, time freedom, and fun?"* I was pretty surprised to learn that most people are not interested in even taking a glance at network marketing.

You might as well know now that this "innovator/early adopter" group of 16 percent feels quite unreachable when you start your journey with network marketing. On rare occasions, a new distributor will have "beginner's luck" and find a "blue M&M" right out of the gate. They will then spend the next six months to a year thinking they've lost their touch, because they just cannot seem to find another one. They will ask again and again, "What am I doing wrong?" It's important to remember that a full 84 percent of the people you contact will say, "No, not now" or "No, never". If this is the case, I ask you, how important is it to learn the art of following up and closing? The answer is simple and powerful. It is imperative. It is life or death in network marketing. It means success or failure.

I know one thing for sure. If you do not ask, recruiting will not happen. Imagine a young man wanting to go to the homecoming dance and never asking a young woman to accompany him. I suppose there might be an occasional brave gal who would extend an invitation, but I suggest that this would be an exception and not the norm. Similarly, it is highly unlikely that anyone will ever accost you to join your network marketing business.

I am thinking back to a time when my children were one and three years old. We lived in Michigan, and I was thirty-seven years old. I loved my boys with all my heart and still missed the freedom and activity of my life before kids. It was cold, and we spent a lot of time inside. Gordon had a new job and worked long hours, and I knew almost nobody. My friend Ginny was a lifeline. She had two little boys as well and had just moved to Michigan from the same small town as me: San Clemente, California. She enjoyed working out and was involved in a direct selling company that featured scrapbooking. I was hardly the scrapbooking type. I was "action girl". I played tennis and took Spinning classes. I rarely slowed down. I took pictures of my family and my life and threw them into a box.

Scrapbooking became an outlet for me. I was creative, and I loved my family. I loved the idea of showcasing my little boys and their activities. It became an obsession of mine. I would put the boys down for a nap and blast down to the basement to my little workshop and get lost in cutting, pasting, and creating. I often wondered if I could get the materials any cheaper and what commissions might be offered if I shared what I was doing with others. I often thought of asking Ginny about the financial payoff for what she did but never got around to it. My husband had a great job, and I was pretty busy with my fitness activities.

I can tell you now, after two decades in the business, that I could have been greatly successful in that company. You see, I was unlike any other rep with whom I came in contact. I threw ten pages together in one day! I ripped the paper, shaped the photos, and slapped them onto the page. I was innovative and used colored paper backgrounds and stickers for interest, with very little thought at all. The other moms I watched cut slowly and meticulously but got very little done. They used far fewer materials than I did and never got the traction I got in every session. I did a whole page in just a few minutes and never saw anyone move the way I did in creating a scrapbook. To this day I feel confident I could have taught classes on how to go fast and get a lot done. I could have sold lots of supplies and taught those women how to showcase their memories in a matter of hours—not days, weeks, and months. That company needed me: my passion, my system, and my style. My albums were gorgeous. They were interesting and fun.

Scrapbooking filled a need for me for the two years I was raising babies who had to have a nap every single day whether I was ready to stop or not. I believe I would have sold more paper, scissors, stickers, and albums than any other woman in the history of that company. I do not say that to boast or brag. I was driven. I was a long way from home and lonely. I was bored during naptime. I believe I could have been the best "rep" that company had ever seen. I will never know what could have been. Why? Ginny never asked me to join her company. I loved that woman and still do. She is a remarkable mother, entrepreneur, and friend. I have never told her how much I thought about that potential career. I had little confidence. I did not ask her if I could join her team. I often wonder where she and I would be if she had invited me to partner with her in the business. She just never asked me to that dance.

My kids were in elementary school when I got facials once a month from my friend Jane. Again, raising those little boys felt stifling at times. I adored them but often could not wait for a bit of adult conversation and especially a laugh with a friend. Jane was funny, and I do not know how she ever did my facials, because we never stopped talking or laughing. I knew she was a distributor for a high-end skin-care company because she dropped hints all the time about her new business and products. I was mildly curious, even though skin care was not of high value to me at the time. I was relatively young and clueless and just learning the value of taking care of my skin. She would go on and on about how important it was to cleanse, exfoliate, and moisturize. She was passionate about the products she was using. I waited and waited for her to ask me to join her in her new endeavor. I figured it would likely be $200 or more to buy the starter kit, and I just was not going to volunteer to spend that money. However, I had made a decision. If and when she asked me, I would not say no. She never asked—true story. She just did not have the confidence to invite me to join her business. She incorrectly assumed that I would not be interested since my husband had a good job. She assumed I would invite myself to join her if I was interested in getting the products. She was a bit embarrassed and nervous about admitting that she was part of a direct selling company. She was dead wrong. I spent $1,100 to join that company just a few years later. I stayed in long enough to recruit my best prospect—a woman who went on to have giant success in that business. This gal could have set Jane free. Instead of doing facials, she might have become a giant success in network marketing. If only. Maybe. Shoulda', coulda', woulda'. Do not be that person who doesn't buck up and ask! You will never know what it might cost you.

Some years later I was having tea in the home of a new friend when she pulled out a "farmhouse basket" and began to poke flowers into the various holes to decorate it. It went from simple and functional to being a professional-looking bouquet in a matter of five minutes. I asked her where she was going and how she had learned to *do that*. She shrugged it off and told me she was going to a party. I pressed her for more information, asking if the arrangement was a gift for the hostess. I wanted to know what kind of a party she was attending. She was vague and changed the subject. I finally gleaned that she was going to a party and would be offering products from the catalog that was sitting on the counter. I began to flip through it and offered, "I will have a party for you." I told her I would love to have some free stuff. She was quiet and noncommittal, and I pushed her by asking, "So if I sign up, could I have the free stuff plus the commissions?"

She said, "Sure, we can do that." I begged her to sign me up right then and there. I accosted her for catalogs and a date. I remember it like it was yesterday. I wanted that farmhouse basket and many other things her company offered, and I secretly imagined teaching other women to do what I was going to do.

To this day, my sponsor in that company remains one of my favorite people on this planet. She is smart, generous, and funny. If I had not begged to join her business, we would not have gone on to build two successful businesses together. In fact, I do not believe we would have built our friendship either. As our friend Dr. Seuss says, "Oh, the places you'll go!" To that I say, "Not if you do not *ask!*"

People want to be skillfully led. They want to be invited. If they are not interested, they will tell you no, and it hurts only if you are attached to the answer. Here is what I know for sure: If you do not *ask*, people will not join you. And you must ask *again and again*, because most people do not say yes until after the fifth exposure.

Be brave. Be courageous. If you are not fearless, you will never know the magnitude of what you may be leaving on the table.

THE LANGUAGE OF VENUS

Every profession has its own jargon and distinct language. Each profession has a group of unique expressions used by the insiders. In real estate and mortgage you will hear terms such as *refi*, *buy down, equity, APR,* and *amortization.* As brokers and agents glibly use these terms, it can be confusing for their new clients and thus hinder clear communication.

In my fitness career we used jargon amongst ourselves and with our clients. We learned and shared the concepts of body composition, VO2 Max, Fartlek and interval training, aerobic and anaerobic activity, repetitions and sets, and maximum and target heart rates. Throwing these terms around without educating our clients was probably intimidating and counterproductive to the people we served.

To this day I remember the jargon used when I was waitressing and bartending my way through college. *Four top on two* meant that I had four people on table two who needed attention. *Eighty-six baked potatoes* meant that we were out of potatoes until further notice. Getting *stiffed* meant that I hadn't received a tip for my service. For years after I stopped working in restaurants I had nightmares about getting *slammed* and finding myself *in the weeds*. I submit to you, however, that jargon is necessary, required, and here to stay, even though it tends to separate the insiders from the outsiders. In network marketing, we are all about inclusion. Being mindful of our use of jargon can certainly improve our overall communications, and that is a good thing.

I am dedicating an entire section to network marketing jargon because I would like to see a massive overhaul in the "languaging" of our beautiful profession. I believe we must set the example of speaking correctly early on with our new business partners. We must not wait until they have been around for a year or more and then try to undo what we have created. Let me take a moment and make this point using my little Venusians as an illustration.

I remember a time when Iain was two years old and in a rage. He yelled, "I hate you, Mom!" My reaction was swift, calm, and immediate. I knelt down to his level, looked into his eyes from six inches away, held on to both of his hands, and told him, "You can be frustrated, and you may even raise your voice. You may express your irritation and anger. However, you may never, ever say, 'I hate you' again. This is not language to be used with anyone, and certainly not with the people you love." Simple. Concise. Firm. He never did it again, because he knew I was serious. He learned early on that I would not tolerate abusive and inappropriate language.

While our kids were small, we reinforced a number of changes with them. Instead of "I want it" or "Gimme' it" we asked them to use "May I please have it?" They would tell us yes or no when asked if they wanted more food, a play date, or a toy. We immediately let them know that "Yes" or "No" was not enough. It always needed to be "No, thank you" or "Yes, please". We taught them to say, "It is nice to meet you" and "It is nice to see you again." They learned how to look people in the eye and deliver a firm—but not bone-breaking—handshake. You are probably asking yourself, *"What does this have to do with network marketing?"*

When I enroll a new distributor, I feel like I have birthed a child. I take it *seriously*. Just like my kids, this person is a reflection of *me*, of the tribe, and of the Company. I feel personally responsible for showing them the ropes and for teaching them how to speak and behave on Venus. I recognize that I am not their mother, and I am not their boss. However, I am a role model, and I take that job to heart. Just like teaching our boys how to communicate effectively with our family, their teachers, and their peers, I am going to do my best to see that my new distributor learns the right way to communicate for the greatest success in network marketing.

Let's talk about something that most of us use every day before we discuss some of the words that may alienate a new person checking out your Company for the first time, inside and outside our business world: the euphemism.

A euphemism is a mild or indirect word or expression that is substituted for one that is considered too harsh or blunt. I am not embarrassed to be involved in network marketing. I am not ashamed of our remarkable profession. I am sure you have gathered how passionate I am about this business model that has set my family free. I do, however, know that its name has been dragged through the mud. It will take some time and commitment to shift the view of our lovely business model. I believe euphemisms are of tremendous value in our business.

First, let's talk about the term *network marketing*. To be honest, I really do not use it when I am talking to someone about my business for the first time. When I am in front of a room, I use the term *person-to-person distribution* or *word-of-mouth advertising*. You may ask why; I do it because it is a bit softer. It is a way of introducing our system and business model that is more palatable. I have found that *word-of-mouth* or *person-to-person* is a softer and warmer way to introduce people to our world. The door stays open a little wider. The mind remains open long enough to receive pertinent information for the decision-making process. Sometimes people attend an in-home presentation without knowing they are going to hear about a business opportunity. Softer terms are less threatening and give people permission to listen without judgment.

Nothing will turn a guest off faster than terms like *prospect, recruiting,* or *rank.* If network marketing is new to them, these terms are often abrasive and off-putting. Here are some of my ideas on better choices when speaking the "language" of Venus.

Downline is a term used when referring to anyone who joins your line of sponsorship after you do and as a result of your having said "Yes". I much prefer to use and hear the words *organization, group,* or *team.* Remember—TEAM is also an acronym for "together everyone achieves more". Isn't that beautiful?

The term *upline* refers to anyone who joined the business before you, and in the same line of sponsorship. I prefer to hear people talk about the person who enrolled them, the friend who shared the business with them, or the one who brought them to the Company. When you are hanging around with a bunch of network marketers, these terms are not so offensive. However, when a brand new person is present, they may feel uncomfortable when hearing about their *upline,* their *downline,* and the *ranks.*

Be careful when you use the word *prospect.* I would not want my best friend or mother to call me one. I like to refer to my friends, family members, and colleagues as *potential business partners.* I think they would resonate more with that as well. If you have a "new recruit", remember this is not the army! How about identifying them as a new colleague, teammate, business partner, friend, or associate when introducing them to others?

Be conscious when you are trying to find out where someone fits or is situated in your Company. Do not say, "Whose leg are you in?" or "Who got you in?" Rather, ask, "Who invited you here today?" or "How did you learn about this Company?" You might tell people, "I am a part of Terry's organization" or "Jim shared this amazing opportunity with me a few months ago."

Do not ask people, "When did you sign up" or "When did you get in?" It is much softer to ask, "When did you join the Company?" or "How long have you and Dave been business partners?" If guests are nearby and listening (and they are always nearby and listening if your business is growing), it is important to set a good example by making good word choices.

Consider this. A man may speak one way when eating dinner with his family at the dinner table. He may let his hair down when having a beer with the guys. If women are sitting around the table having tea and the kids come in, it's likely the conversation will shift a little to become a bit more kid-friendly. So let's be conscious of who is listening when we are participating in "shop talk" at opportunity meetings, trainings, and our events. Be cognizant of everyone in the area, even if they are not in your organization. You are not just representing yourself. You are also a reflection of the Company as well as the profession at large. Words are strong. Words have energy. On Venus we use words that elevate, unify, and inspire, not words that divide and alienate others. Words can cut and cause wounds that cannot be seen. Once words leave your mouth, they are out there. They cannot be taken back. Be the change you want to see in network marketing. Choose wisely. Be conscious. Be inclusive. Be a great example.

11

THE VENUS VIEW OF KIDS

ONCE UPON A TIME I was a mother for whom the title of this chapter would have incited guilt and shame. I used to nitpick myself to death and worry that my kids were "missing out" on *me*. Today, I am proud and excited to write a chapter dedicated to the next generation of Venusians in our lives. My Venusians are sixteen and eighteen years old and six foot three and six foot one respectively. Yet they need me as much today as they ever did.

I am writing this chapter because I have a unique perspective. I built a direct selling business before Iain and Cameron were born. My husband worked full-time. I built another business when the boys were five and seven years old. I built a successful business and reached the top of a company when the boys were nine and eleven, while my husband traveled internationally for his job. And I began to build my current multimillion-dollar-per-month business when the boys were ten and twelve, after my husband retired from his job. I know the worries and concerns that can consume you. I know the choices that you are making as you yearn for free time and financial security and what that will afford you in the future.

First, let me assure you that you do *not* have the corner on the market when it comes to fear, remorse, and anxiety over raising a family as a network marketing professional. If you are not feeling these emotions, you have either gone through the process of identifying, sorting through, and managing them and find yourself in a "healthy place" or you are in complete denial and might just live on Mars. I will let you decide for yourself. This chapter certainly is not meant to create guilt but rather to put this "kid stuff" into perspective. Take what works and leave the rest, just as I hope you have done throughout this entire book.

If you are reading this book, highlighting and taking notes, and thinking about with whom you are going to share it, the chances are good that you are a "driver". It is quite possible that you are a bit obsessed with your business and that you lose sleep analyzing and planning. To tell you the truth, I lost sleep for many years. I was either building my business, thinking about building my business, or stressing out about *not* building my business. I wish I could save you from that trap, but I believe it is in the DNA of any successful and passionate network marketer. I have found prayer and meditation to be helpful in keeping me in alignment with my family and my purpose, but it took me years to avail myself of those practices. Perhaps you will start now. Perhaps you will connect in the morning with your inner self and reach out and up to the higher power of your choosing and ask, "Where can I be of service today?" I sincerely recommend it. Breathing through this process will save your adrenal glands, which is important. Some of you will, and some of you won't. Quiet time is good. Quiet time will channel your energies in positive and constructive ways. Venusians love these fifteen to twenty minutes of peace and solitude. If you do it, it will help you. It will help you to help your family.

I am going to start this conversation with a story that I have shared for years and years from my own business journey. It still makes me laugh. I was sitting with a mom from one of my boys' sports teams, sharing my story about the business. It is likely that I was not as effective as I am today. It is possible that I was giving her a presentation and not finding out what she did not have in her life that she wanted deeply. I doubt that I spent much time asking her if she was ready to do something about it. I believe I might have been living on Mars at the time. At any rate, we had been together for about an hour when I finished my canned presentation with a closing question like "Are you ready to join me in building a business?"

She looked at me with a straight face and said, "I cannot build a business, Carrie. I have kids." That was the end of the conversation. I had no place to go from there and nothing to say. She knew I had children and that Gordon traveled the world.

What she did not know was that I had gone through gyrations just two days before to get my boys situated so I could do an in-home presentation thirty minutes from my home. It was about four o'clock, and I was making calls. I was in sweats and a comfortable sweatshirt, UGG boots, and a hat (my business building uniform for winter) when I glanced at the clock. I almost had a heart attack. My kids had soccer practices one in one city and the other in another. I had to feed them, get them ready for practice, find rides home for them, get myself ready for an in-home presentation, and then get on the road.

I ran to the neighbors' home with two towels, two blankets, two pillows, and two stuffed animals. I asked her if I could drop the boys by her place after their respective practices. I brought the boys with me, laid out the towels on her toy room floor, and showed them where they would go to sleep after dinner. I pointed to each cute little bed and said, "This is your bed, Iain, and Cameron, this one is yours. Slumber party, woo-hoo!" I asked my neighbor to feed the kids the food I had brought and said I would swing by around ten and walk them down to our house and put them to bed. I then called a few moms from the kids' teams and arranged rides from the soccer fields to our neighbors' home.

Now, I am not suggesting that I would receive the Mother of the Year award for this slick maneuver, and it is not something I did every week. I suggest that you will not get to the top of your Company, change lives, and build a successful business without some sacrifices, quick thinking, and acting.

I opened my neighbor's door that night around ten, woke my little boys, and grabbed the bedding, and we trudged down the street. I kissed their noses and prayed that I had not scarred them for life. The whole walk home I thought, *"Yep, I can do this, because I've got kids!"*

What's the bottom line? On Venus, we do not make our kids our excuse; we make them our reason. We do not hope things happen; we make them happen!

I love my boys every bit as much as that cute mom loved hers. I am just wired for business, and I have the *will* to find the *way*. My "why" burns inside of me. It is for my family that I use creative planning to follow my dreams. Yes, moms and dads *can* build a business, even if the other is not in the picture for the day or forever. Nobody said it was going to be easy. On Venus we tell the truth. I am telling you it is difficult but not impossible. I am also telling you that it is *worth it*.

One thing I know for sure. Network marketing provides a laboratory for personal growth. Your kids are watching you and learning from all you *say* and do. They observe each "chemical reaction" with interest. They make mental notes each time there is an experiment. They observe frustration, excitement, anxiety, joy, empathy, compassion, anger, sadness, and enthusiasm. More important, they learn how to handle each of those feelings. Network marketing promises a myriad of teaching opportunities along the road to success. A smart man or woman will use some of this real-life research in enriching the character of their Venusian offspring. I often say, aloud and to myself "Your actions speak so loudly, I cannot hear a word you are saying." In life and in network marketing, your kids and your business partners do not pay a whole lot of attention to what you say unless you back it up with what you *do*.

I giggle as I recall a "lab experiment" that Cherise, my beautiful friend and business partner, conducted when her boys Christopher and Luke were four and seven. She was on the phone, building her business from her kitchen, when a skirmish broke out. Her boys were loud, and the argument was becoming physical. The call she was on was important. She quickly excused herself and got between the furious, flailing little Martians. She reminded them that they were brothers, that they loved each other, and that they lived on Venus. She informed them that she was building her business and needed their help and cooperation. She also admonished them for their dangerous interaction. She said something like "If you want to get close to each other, I can help you with that!" She then proceeded to "duct-tape" them together in a hugging position.

Honestly, Cherise and I have had some long and loud laughing episodes, but this one took the cake. What more is there to say? This lab experiment is one they will never forget; neither will the thousands who have received her message on stage and via audiotapes. Mama took a stand. Mama made a point. Mama made it a teaching moment and provided a valuable lesson: awesome mama.

If you are building a business, you are likely remembering many such interactions with your own children or with someone else's. You have likely had these frustrating opportunities for growth in your world if you are a mom or dad, aunt, uncle, grandparent, or babysitter. There is much that can be taught, and there is much to be learned as well. One of the biggest problems I see in network marketing, as in any other profession, is putting kids on the proverbial back burner for years. There are two words to describe my feelings on this move: not okay. Your kids are resilient and adaptable. They will survive your lack of attention and participation in their lives. It will be *you* who may suffer with guilt and remorse down the road. It is not necessarily how *much* time you are able to give your children every day. It is how present you make yourself during those precious moments. Learn to turn off your phone and computer when they get up in the morning. Be ready with a tray of healthful snacks when your kids walk in the door from school. Hang out with them for fifteen minutes around the dinner table and ask them about their day and *listen* to what they share with you.

Oprah once did a show on parenting children; her expert guest taught something I have never forgotten. She advised us to be *delighted* when our children enter the room. Rather than rolling our eyes because the nap was too short or the TV show is over or they have come home early from a play date, be joyful that they have walked into your world for yet another moment. You may have to fake it until you make it on this one, but I have found it to be extremely beneficial to my boys and me. If you are mindful about it and make it a routine, your little ones will look forward to it. Take the last minute or two to remind them that you work from home so that you can put the Band-Aid on if they fall and cuddle them if they have a temperature and have to stay home. Let them know that you have a job and that you have chosen to have your office at home because you love and care about them. Remind them that it is time for you to get back to your business; that they must do their homework and play nicely per your agreement. If you take this high-quality time with them and really *connect* with them, they will be able to amuse themselves for the next hour or two. Hold this healthy boundary each and every day and make the special time sacred. Try it. You'll like it and so will they!

You may have heard the quote by Benjamin Franklin that goes like this: "Tell me and I forget, teach me and I may remember, involve me and I learn." Network marketing is an excellent way to teach our kids about many values and experiences. Commitment, fear, tenacity, disappointment, perseverance, goals, partnership, sharing, planning, and rewards are all threads in the network marketing tapestry. Giving our children real-life examples and involving them in our business-building practices will give them more than they will ever receive in any classroom.

I have business partners that I admire greatly for the way they have included their beautiful little girls in building their networking business and their future. Shawn and Michelle have stellar habits and work consistently to help others reach their goals in network marketing. They are selfless and tireless in their pursuit of freedom, creating a family environment that is healthy and productive for each of its members. Michelle and Shawn have a beautiful, young, live-in nanny who loves their children and has become a member of their tribe. She does the housework, cooking, shopping, and cleaning so that Michelle and Shawn can do their job of building their network.

Here's the cool part. The girls are part of the team. They have family goals and rewards that are visible in their home. They have charts and graphs written on the walls of the master bathroom that they use to record their progress. They have short-term goals like getting ice cream as a family. The longer-term goals have included a Disney cruise and an African safari. Those are goals they have reached! The girls know exactly what they are working toward at all times, and they hold their parents accountable.

I remember a time when Shawn and Michelle called me and were quite distraught. They had been building their business for about two solid years and were struggling with the fact that they were preparing to take a two-week vacation with their family. They wondered if they were missing the mark by being away from their business and completely out of touch. They were not sure if the "short-term imbalance for long-term balance" meant they should forgo all travel and time with extended family and wait for a point in the future when they had "arrived". I get this question a lot and am extremely passionate about answering it. It is simple, clear, and all Venusian: *Life is what happens to you while you are making your plans.* I told my friends to relish the time they had set aside to enjoy their parents and their girls. I told them to shut off and shut down and let their team members "step in and step up". I reminded them that kids want to go to Disneyland and take trips with their parents when they are seven and nine years old—not typically when they are fifteen- and seventeen-year-old teenagers.

None of us has a crystal ball, and no one among us has any idea when we will take our last breath. What we *can* be sure of is that our kids are going to grow up. If we have done our job right, they will leave us and create a life and a family of their own. Building a strong and solid network marketing business with walk-away residual income will not usually be accomplished in just a few years, especially if it is your first go-round. I urge you to work diligently when you are working. I also suggest that you learn to play like your life depends on it. Learn to turn on. Be confident and comfortable turning off when it is required. If you are your business, you will never be free to step out when and if you need to. Practice the discipline of resting and rejuvenating. Plan for it. Relish it. Share it with your team when you return, and thank them for their part in making it a reality. Then get back to work with commitment, power, and passion.

Always remember that people are watching you (Especially your kids!) They are observing all that you do. They are deciding every single day whether they want what you have. They are watching what you are creating for yourself. If you do not inspire them by the life you are leading, they will hesitate to follow in your footsteps.

I will wrap this chapter up with a few thoughts on what I would do differently if I could go back. After all, I did promise to give you some ideas on how to avoid the pitfalls and mistakes that I have made along the way.

I wish I had talked on the phone less when my boys were in the car. Knowing what I know now, I would have taken fewer calls when I was driving them to and from school. That time was incredible for communicating, connecting, and catching up. Some days I assumed they would be little forever. If I had it to do again, I would choose to take a call only when it was imperative.

I would have been less frantic when they interrupted. The "I am on the pho-o-o-ne" look got old and lost its power. They countered with "Mom, you're *always* on the phone." I would have created twenty-minute blocks of time when I turned off and tuned in to them. Back then it seemed like the end of the world if I did not pick up the phone for my distributors and prospects. I recognize today that a really interested person will still be really interested twenty minutes later. I wish I hadn't been so rigid.

I will finish with a story from my two-year stint as a corporate wife and mother of two toddlers in Northville, Michigan. I remember being in a department store with my boys. A mature woman watched me struggling to get them both going in the same direction on the escalator. She looked at me with a wise and understanding smile and said, "I know it is frustrating, dear. Just remember—the days go slowly, but the years go fast." My goodness, how right she was.

Parenthood is a privilege. Your kids are not yours. They come *through* you and then they are gone. When they are small, you are the center of their world. They yearn for your time, your attention, and your love. Network marketers are not the only parents who wonder, *"When did they get taller than me? When did they get so big?"* But I believe that networkers have more choices than most. Choose your children. Read to them. Walk with them. Cook with them, even if it is just for twenty minutes a few times per week. They will remember it, and so will you.

You have heard it said, "It is not the destination, it is the journey." I could not agree more. Consider who you are becoming, and learn to manage your business, your family, and yourself. Last thing: If and when you have teenagers, definitely make them feel important by turning off your phone while you're in the car. It sends a powerful message.

12

THE RISE OF THE FEMININE IN NETWORK MARKETING

I HAVE WAITED MANY YEARS to write this important chapter. None is more pertinent. A shift in the culture of direct selling and network marketing is under way. It's needed and long over due. Network marketing is beautiful. Network marketing is fair. Network marketing makes sense. It attracts some of the finest men and women on the planet. Unfortunately, it also provides a feeding ground for those who are not yet aware—those who still believe in lack and limitation. These "asleep people" have bloodied and battered the reputation of a lovely business model, a winning concept. It is not irreversible, however. It is time for all "light workers" to beam the profession with joy, compassion, empathy, and hope. Bringing network marketing out of the darkness and into the light is the responsibility of each of us.

According to the Direct Selling Association (www.dsa.org) a full 80 percent of the people who join direct selling and network marketing in the United States alone are women. Women love to talk. Women love to share. An "awake" woman loves to lift others, to laugh, and to love. However, many women are afraid to lead. In network marketing, there are very few women speaking from the stage. Some are terrified to expose their imperfections and live in fear of being "found out". Inside they shudder and say to themselves, *"If you really knew me, you would be disappointed, put off, or even disgusted. I must remain undercover if I am to survive."* If we are going to make a permanent shift in the culture of this business model, we must awaken one another to the feminine energy that resides within us all, men and women alike. We must own the shadowy parts of our personalities, including the parts that frighten us.

Women are not alone in their fear of being "discovered". Men struggle, usually in complete silence. They too wonder, *"Am I enough? Am I worthy? Do I measure up? Am I a real man? A real man would not be so scared."* When I speak about the rise of the feminine, I implore my male readers to hear my invitation to grow. Throughout my journey I have been touched to my core by the authentic, raw, and real sharing of men as they open to the process of their own unveiling.

What does it mean to light the way for the travelers coming on our heels? What do I mean as I implore each of you to embrace your inner warrior for peace, love, and truth? Let me lay it out for you. Let me share my thoughts about how network marketing looks on Venus.

First, though, let's take another look at the latest statistics provided by the Direct Selling Association's website. In 2013 the direct selling sales force in the United States alone was made up of approximately 16.8 million people. A total of 13.8 percent of US households had a direct seller in them. Further, the 2013 estimated retail sales of network marketing products in the United States alone were $32.67 billion. Because of the decline in corporate America and the difficulties faced in the US economy in the last couple of years, I believe these numbers are much, much higher today. As you can see, these numbers are not small. Network marketing is not going away. Rather, it is taking root and gaining momentum. Since this is the case, it is imperative that we guard and protect this profession and "shine it up" for ourselves and for those who need it so desperately: newcomers to the profession.

In contemplating how to start a conversation of this magnitude, I ask myself, *"Where do I begin to discuss the culture shift that is so needed in network marketing?"* The answer comes quickly. Once upon a time, an admirer asked Michelangelo, "How did you carve the *David?*"

He replied, "I just looked at the giant slab of marble and removed anything and everything that was not David in order to reveal him." I believe it will be helpful if I follow that model and explain what network marketing looks like at its best by stripping away those aspects that give it the proverbial black eye. I believe it is important to tell you what network marketing is *not*. In doing so, I hope to reveal everything that it can be.

Network marketing is not about "getting one". It is not about making money on someone. It is about finding like-minded entrepreneurs who are looking for what you are offering. Network marketing is not about aggressively badgering your friends, neighbors, family, and coworkers to get in. It is about offering a vehicle by which to achieve time and financial freedom through consistent, concerted effort over time. As I have said before, people expect too much too soon in this profession. It is no different from any other profession out there. It takes years to have big success in networking. There are disappointments along the way, and sometimes they are huge. You may be with a few companies before you "hit," just like in real estate, insurance, franchising, or owning your own business.

Network marketing is not about exaggerating and lying as a means of attracting people to the business. A responsible network marketer tells the truth. It is not fair to promise too much too soon. It is not kind to give people false expectations. I have gone so far as to tell a potential business partner that network marketing is a bit like looking for a needle in a haystack. When you begin, it can seem like you are the only one on the planet who sees the vision. One day, though, as you are learning your craft, honing your skills, going from an "unconscious incompetent" to an "unconscious competent," you will find someone who grabs on to the vision like you did. Suddenly there are two of you looking for that needle. With just one more person looking, it may not seem much faster although it is usually more fun. It may still feel like you will never find it. Then there will be three or four of you sifting and sorting, working through the haystack. One day there will be six, then ten, and then twenty-five people looking for that precious needle. Pretty soon—and maybe it will be a year or more—you will find that needle, and it will be time to move on to another haystack.

What exactly is the "needle" in network marketing? It is your "locker". It is a person who comes into your business, usually many generations down, that gets it, *really* gets it. They dig in. They duplicate what you do. They do everything that is required. They shock you and sometimes intimidate you with their tenacity and fearlessness. They are like a dog with a bone. They will do it because they must do it. They may not be the fastest, the brightest, or the most obvious choice, but they are with you for the long haul. They have seen the light, and they will not settle for the darkness. It is as if they are in a one-way tunnel. The light may or may not be visible ahead, but it is definitely dark where they have come from, and they are not going back. This person will lead you to many, many more like them: passionate and committed people who are yearning for something more.

Network marketing is not about owning or controlling others. You are a free agent, bound only by the policies and procedures of your chosen company. You are an independent business owner, and so are the people you enroll. Your best strategy is to become a student of the profession, a student of your Company's system, a student of people, and, most importantly, a student of yourself.

The concept of duplication is something you will hear constantly in the profession of network marketing. You will also hear the word *duplicatable*, which is not a word. The word is *duplicable*, and I have waited two decades to point this out. Although nobody has a boss in network marketing, we all need leaders, mentors, and teachers to help us on our journeys. Although the concepts of control and ownership have no place in networking, duplication is essential. The point I am trying to make is to be the leader and mentor that you want. Encourage and teach duplication as often as possible. Whereas Martians (and Martians can be women) seek to control others, to be in charge and insist that people fall into line behind them, a Venusian uses the law of attraction in building their business. Venusians know that like attracts like and that you must become the person you hope to attract. Building a team is like building a volunteer army; you are constantly working to attract your "generals". You will not do this by force, but by being the example. Your positive energy and empathy will be magnetic. People will be drawn to what you are building. Remember people are watching you. They are deciding if they want what you have. Over time, they will join you if you are becoming what they want to become.

Network marketing is not about being exclusive. It is not about drawing lines and boundaries and being fearful about sharing precious secrets with the people in other lines of sponsorship. Venusians don't wallow in the fear of not having enough of the market. I must admit, there were times when I struggled with the concept of "A rising tide raises all boats." When I embraced leadership, I struggled with the idea of training everyone else's team. I was raising two small children and trying to be a good wife and mother. I was committed to staying fit and to keeping in close touch with my friends and extended family. It seemed counterproductive working with other people's people—or at least an expenditure of precious energy in a way that was diluting my efforts for my team. I have come to learn that this selfish or controlling attitude is one of the most destructive aspects of our beautiful business model. Just like in life, it will destroy the fabric of a culture and a community.

Now, I am not suggesting that you must do home meetings and three-way calls for everyone in the Company. What I *am* suggesting is that you remember that you are building a *company* and the reputation of a *profession* as well as your team. If you are training or leading a conference call, what on earth will it hurt to have other people listening in and receiving inspiration and motivation to go out and spread the good news about your Company and its products? If you are having a community-building event, I encourage you to include everyone in the area when possible, whether or not they fall under your business "umbrella". Some people are shuddering as they read these words. A Martian will say things like "I can't have everyone in my living room" or "I'm paying for that hotel room, and we can only fit a hundred people!" They will continue with "I am not going to train other people's teams to take market share. It does not make good business sense!" These are dangerous and archaic thoughts anchored in lack and limitation. They challenge the growth and integrity of our business model. Believe me—"What goes around comes around" has never been more universal than right here and right now in this conversation. I cannot tell you how many times I have helped a person from another team, only to learn how much I have been blessed in the process. I could give you example after example. Sometimes the perfect cross-line person will show up and say just the right thing to my potential business partner, and they join my business on the spot. I have had random people show up hither and thither who are able to help me with a technology problem or a malfunctioning DVD player or projector. If they were dropped into the room by a fairy godmother, it could not have seemed more perfect. It's on those occasions that I give the most that I am richly blessed, and when I least expect it.

It is time for all of us to help network marketing "grow up". In many companies today, distributors act like toddlers fighting over toys as if they are two years old.

"That's my truck and you can't play with it!" "It doesn't matter that I have a room full of toys, I want the one that *you* are playing with *now*!"

"This is my team, and you're not invited to participate! I don't want to share my secrets with you, because if I do, you might sponsor my neighbor or friend!"

The reason I am so passionate about this topic is that there was a time when I was fearful and tired. I was afraid that helping the entire Company would somehow diminish my "foothold" and take away from my family, friends, and fitness. I was dead wrong.

I am not suggesting that boundaries are not important. I have learned how to say no when I must. I have learned to send people to a resource, to another person, or to a book for training and inspiration. I certainly cannot be all things to all people, and neither can you. When I am getting out of balance in my life, I will say something like this:

I would help each and every one of you in this Company with three-way calls and in-home meetings if I could. I wish I could be everywhere for everyone. The reality is that I have two teenagers who need me. I am committed to being a good wife to my husband and a good mother to my boys. I must exercise each day and have quiet time for prayer and meditation in the morning. I need to stay in close touch with my mother, who lives close by. There are times when I have to choose between doing a three-way call and hanging out with them. I know you will understand when I tell you that I must choose my family.

I can honestly tell you I have never had even one person not understand wholeheartedly. I will always follow with something like this:

Let me tell you what I can do. I can give you a few people whom you can call to introduce yourself and see if you have a connection. They would likely be happy to do three-way calls with you if you offer to do third-party validation for them. In addition I have a few resources I'd like to send via e-mail that may help you. I can give you a couple of incredible book referrals as well. Remember leaders are readers.

When you attend a meeting, training, or large event, you must reach out to the people right and left of you and make connections. Ask them how they came to join your Company, and then tell them your story. If there is no real bond, reach out to someone else. In this way you will be building relationships and offering and gaining support. This is good practice for the work of meeting new friends and potential business partners in your everyday life. These venues are full of positive and excited people who will help you become better!

Building a culture is like building a family. Gordon and I are doing our best to raise our boys to be empathetic, polite, chivalrous, helpful, and outgoing, with good work ethics and strong morals. Frankly, it is a huge job, and we cannot do it all by ourselves. You have heard it said, "It takes a village." I believe this to be true. Ministers, teachers, coaches, Boy Scout troop leaders, other kids' parents, grandparents, neighbors, aunts, and uncles are all part of the mix. What parent feels adequate to be all things at all times to their kids? I don't know any.

Network marketing is no different. Our profession is coming of age. It's time for us to reach out like those adults who are generously weaving the fabric of our children's character. Help and inspire another from the very beginning, and it will be comfortable when you are "big fish" in our business. Be kind. Be helpful. Be open and willing to help. It will pay you. I promise. It is the law of reciprocity, and its job is to shower you with everything you want and need. What you give out comes back to you, pressed down, multiplied, and magnified: Simple, beautiful, required on Venus.

There will be people—and even some leaders—who join your business and struggle with this concept. Be patient. Be the example. Do not try to control them. Do not embarrass them or make them wrong. Give them the time and space to come to it. Just as we allow our children to make choices and decisions that are right and sometimes wrong, we must allow our fellow network marketers the freedom to learn these lessons by themselves.

This is a great opportunity to share a story from my own career. It changed me. I was new to a company after having had big success in another one. In other words, I came in as a leader. I began to have meetings and trainings and community-building events, and our team was growing fast. There was a company-wide calendar on which people posted their events. I had no idea how new and young the company really was. I was under the impression that it was much further along in its growth cycle. I was afraid to post my home meetings on the calendar for fear that a hundred people or more would show up! I had been in the profession for years, and my neighbors had come to my door many times to express concern over the number of cars on the street. They had come to remind me that doing business from home was not allowed in our community.

People in my Company began to notice that I was growing and advancing in rank, yet there were no meetings posted on the calendar. They were frustrated and a bit irritated. It took a few months, but I began to realize that our Company was truly in its infancy and that I was safe posting my events, so I did. It was much later when a member of the corporate staff told me how he handled the situation with the other leaders:

> Carrie comes to us from another company. She comes with history. Let's just pretend we're all back in kindergarten for a minute. We all go to school every day and play on the playground in our blue pants. Carrie comes to us from out of the area, and she's wearing red pants. She continues to come to school for a while wearing her red pants and eventually notices that our uniform is blue. One day Carrie comes to school in blue pants.

End of story. I have loved this guy ever since. He did not make anyone wrong. He did not make anyone or anything right. He told it exactly how it was. The other leaders modeled the right behavior, and I caught on. Today we work together at the top. We post our meetings. We lift each other's people. We work as a team. Venus.

When new people join your Company, show them compassion and grace. Not all company cultures are the same, and you have no idea where they have come from. Corporate America is a whole different animal. It may take a new network marketer a number of years to understand the concept "When I help enough people get what they want, I get what I want." It may be totally different from anything they have ever experienced before.

You may sponsor someone who has come from a cutthroat, competitive background. You may come in contact with a distributor who has never been appreciated or recognized for their professional contributions. Just like in any other arena, people come with the baggage they have collected throughout their lifetimes. So do you. We all have "stuff" we have accumulated. We all have wounds that we are here to heal. Network marketing is a great place to work out our kinks and help others to undo some knots as well. We are all in this together.

As I conclude this conversation on culture and the rise of the feminine, I will finish with a bunch of ideas strung together in no particular order. When we follow these principles, we will reveal a profession that is shiny and new, bulging with hope and promise. When you are feeling mad, sad, irritated, jealous, hurt, forgotten, tricked, confused, envious, wiped out, left out, or depressed, read them for a quick reminder that *you matter*. I hope they will provide a little pick-me-up.

- Be gracious.
- Be patient.
- Be kind.
- Be ethical. If it's 99 percent right, it's 100 percent wrong.
- Don't be "grabby."
- There is enough to go around.
- Trust that if someone is meant to be in your business, they *will* be, and if they are not, they will not be.

- If you lose one here, you will gain one there.
- Always look for the solution that is the highest and best for all involved.
- Keep things in perspective.
- Be transparent.
- Be authentic.
- Own your mistakes.
- Allow people the freedom to be themselves.
- Choose love over fear.
- Never stop learning.
- Be a lifelong student.
- Be an energy maker, not an energy taker—and certainly not an energy breaker.
- "In" joy
- "Faith" it until you make it, and …
- "Peace" it together!

And above all, manage the ego! I believe we will all be better off in network marketing and beyond if we check our egos at the door. *EGO* means "Edging God Out". I have come to know that I do not build my business alone. I am constantly calling on a force greater than myself to put men and women in my path who are looking for change. When I am blessed enough to uncover a gem or even a diamond in the rough, I know that it has been a gift and that I must treat it as such. The ego wants to take credit for everything: a rank advancement, a bonus, a trip, a rockin' new business partner. We yearn to take credit for it all. Remember—in our business, giving the credit elsewhere is always better than basking in the glory. If you get a rank advancement, it is your team that got you there. If you earn a trip, it is their volume that helped you earn it. If you earn a bonus, it's your team's sweat equity that paid you. If you receive a pile of recognition, it is your business partners who got you on the stage. If you procure a new business partner the Universe rewarded you for taking the necessary steps. Do not forget it. You are nothing in network marketing by yourself. The ego is dangerous. Unchecked it will destroy you and your business. Again, I believe it is time for a fundamental shift in the great profession of person-to-person distribution.

At the beginning of the chapter, I talked about the enormous statue *David* that proudly stands in the Uffizi art museum in Florence, Italy. Two men worked on the statue before the white marble was deemed too "imperfect" to complete. (Do you ever feel like that's you? You are just too imperfect to go on in network marketing?) It was twenty-five years before Michelangelo was commissioned to pick up his tools. He worked on it constantly for two years before *David* emerged for the entire world to see. Network marketing is morphing and growing. I believe it is progressing and will be a beautiful place for men and women alike to "time in" as the people God has called them to be. It is going to take time, effort, and intention. You may call me a Pollyanna, but I have a burning desire in my heart to help make network marketing the business that love is building. I fully intend to make it so. Will you help me? Would you like to come to Venus?

About the Author

CARRIE DICKIE IS A WIFE and mother of two boys who never earned more than $40,000 in any calendar year before hitting it big in network marketing in 2008. Carrie graduated from the University of Colorado at Boulder with a degree in Advertising. She always knew what she didn't want to do; she just never knew what she did want to do. Carrie put herself through school waiting tables, bartending, and working as a fitness trainer. After graduation she sold educational materials door-to-door and helped to build a successful fundraising company.

In 1993 Carrie fell into the profession of network marketing. She says, "Working hard is not the only element for success. You have to be at the right place at the right time, and prepared to grow as a person." Network marketing has given Carrie the wealth and freedom to be a wife, mother, daughter, author, motivational speaker, and philanthropist. Carrie says, "I have raised our boys and worked out every day while building an international business from our home. The good news is, you can do it too!!"

Everyone who meets Carrie is called to her light, love, and energy. The magic inside Carrie is that she is deeply called to use her talent for seeing people, loving them, and leading them to their brilliance.

Carrie lives in San Clemente with her husband, Gordon, and their two boys, Iain and Cameron.

EACH OF US IS ON a journey. At times it feels as though we are walking alone, unable to take the next step. Carrie knows how it feels to start at the bottom. She knows what it's like to have fear and self-doubt. She also knows how to overcome it. Carrie stepped into her personal power and is anxious to see you do the same.

As a speaker, author, motivator, and business builder, Carrie's passion and keen wisdom illumine the soul and empower men and women to tap into their own energy and light. As an avid believer in personal development, Carrie has inspired thousands of entrepreneurs to claim their greatness and become the people God has put them here to be. Carrie teaches people to become *fearless*.

Carrie's hope is that you will take hold of the principles in this book, tap into your personal power and joy, and inspire others to shine brightly.